THE BOOK OF
SUPERBIKES

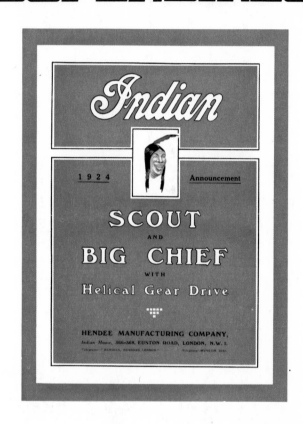

THE BOOK OF
SUPER
BIKES

Mike Winfield
and Laurie Caddell

Published by H.P. Books, P.O. Box 5367, Tucson, AZ 85703
602-888-2150
ISBN 0-89586-067-8
Library of Congress Catalog Card No. 81-81994
©1981 Fisher Publishing, Inc. Printed in U.S.A.

The following have contributed sections to this book: Frank Glendinning (Indian Big Chief, Coventry Eagle, Scott Flying Squirrel, Ariel Square Four, Zündapp K800), Clive Gorman (Norton Dominator, Honda Gold Wing) and Jim Miller (Kawasaki Z1-RTC Turbo, Harley Davidson FLT Tour Glide). The rest of the text has been written by Mike Winfield and Laurie Caddell.

Special thanks to the following people, who either answered questions or gave the names of those who could:

Scott Brown, Harley-Davidson Motorcycles
Brian Casey, BMW Motorrad
Marty Cohen, Iron Horse Motorcycles
Dana Cynaumon, US Suzuki Motor Corp.
Seth Dorfler, Berliner Motor Corp.
Clyde Earl, Webco
Chip Hennen, US Suzuki Motor Corp.
Jacob D. Junker, Indian Motorcycle News
Jane Kress, Kawasaki Motors Corp.
Bob Maggart, Kawasaki of Tucson
Lou Nauert, American Turbo Pak
Herb Ottaway
Robert Runyard, Kawasaki Motors Corp.
Darlene Woo, American Honda Motor Co.
Charles Zimmerman, US Suzuki Motor Corp.

Jim Miller
Editor, US Edition

Editorial Director: Tom Monroe; Art Director: Don Burton; Cover Design: Don Burton, Ken Heiden; Typography; Cindy Coatsworth, Joanne Nociti, Michelle Claridge.

Cover photo by Bill Keller, 1981 BMW R100RS courtesy of Iron Horse Motorcycles.

CONTENTS

FN FOUR

Although preceded by a number of attempts, the first successful application of a four-cylinder engine to a motorcycle was by Fabrique National d'Arme de Guerre, an arms company in Herstal, Belgium. Paul Kelecom of FN put an air-cooled, 362cc straight-four into a tubular frame and developed it for sale in 1904.

In November of that year, an FN development engineer by the name of Osmont set out to test the prototype machine by traversing Europe. In the following weeks he took the machine through France, Italy, Switzerland, Germany, Holland and Belgium and arrived back at the factory near Liege after a flawless journey. Neither rain nor sleet nor dead of night—not even the beginnings of a harsh winter—could stop the bike on its epic trip. Afterwards, however, the machine was regarded by the press as only an expensive curiosity.

Nevertheless, at the Paris Cycle Show the following year that same test bike appeared on the FN stand. The public took to it immediately. Not only was it the first practical four, but it also featured the first successful application of shaft drive—both features which helped to make the bike immensely popular.

When the FN Four was put on sale in Spring, 1905, it featured a 362cc engine of 45 x 55mm bore and stroke, longitudinally mounted in the cradle

The 1921 FN four-cylinder, four-stroke model, which was shaft driven and had a displacement of 750cc.

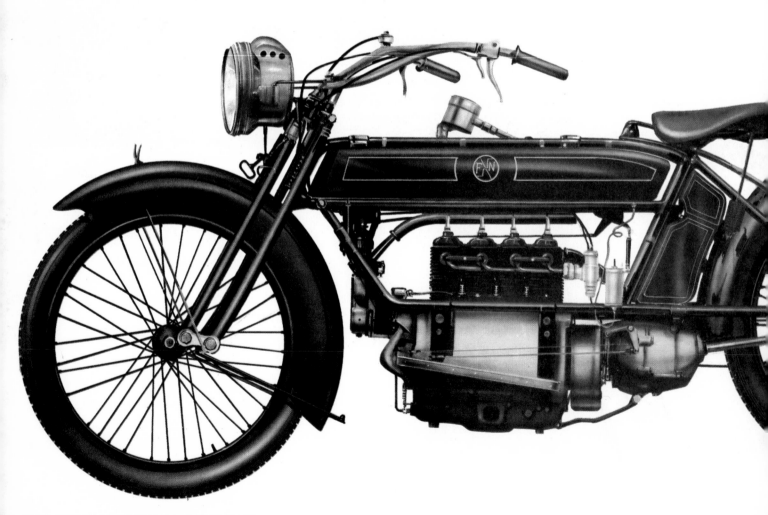

frame. The engine featured five main bearings, automatic (or atmospheric) inlet valves and mechanically operated exhaust valves. A splash lubrication system was used, with individual oil lines running to each connecting-rod well. Ignition was by Simms-Bosch magneto with a separate distributor and was quite reliable for the time. With individual exhaust pipes running from each cylinder to a giant muffler, the FN was so quiet that many who saw one thought that it was steam powered! The sound has also been compared to that of a small, distant aircraft.

The first machines were directly driven, with an all-enclosed ball-bearing shaft drive and no clutch mechanism. A couple of years later, a "free-engine" variation was offered as an option, with a steel-plate clutch provided for easier starting. Instead of being pedaled into motion, the bike could be placed on its rear stand, started and then lowered with the clutch disengaged. The clutch could then be released to get the machine under way. Englishman Sydney Horstmann, later to become famous for his own cars, fitted a two-speed transmission to an FN Four in 1909. Soon after, the company began manufacturing its own two-ratio units.

The first FN Fours weighed just 160 lbs. and their 3 hp engines revved quite freely to a maximum of 1800 rpm, quite a high figure for the time and near

the limit for an automatic-valve arrangement. The top speed of the bike was 35-37 mph, while fuel consumption was very good. The small, four-cylinder engine and shaft drive made the machine remarkably smooth. This, together with the quiet running, made the FN a very popular bike in its day.

Thereafter, the FN grew in size, performance and weight until the end of production with Paul Kelecom's departure in 1926. By that time, however, the shaft drive had been abandoned and the machines featured balloon tires, three-speed gearboxes and electric lighting. These later developments improved both ride and performance so that by the time the model was discontinued in 1926, the maximum speed was a respectable 55 mph.

The engine of a 1906 FN four.

By 1906, the displacement had increased to 498cc.

Inset. The first successful application of shaft final drive was produced by the FN company.

Specification

(1905 model)

engine
Air-cooled, four-stroke, four-cylinder. 45mm (1.77 in.) bore X 55mm (2.17 in.) stroke = 362cc (22 cu.in.). Maximum power 3 bhp at 1800 rpm. Compression ratio not known. Two valves per cylinder, automatic inlet, exhaust operated directly from camshaft. Single Brown & Barlow carburetor

transmission
Single-speed gearbox. Shaft drive

frame
Duplex cradle

suspension
Front - Leading-link/telescopic
Rear - Solid unsprung

brakes
Front - None
Rear - Drum and stirrup

weight
160 lbs. (73kg)

performance
Maximum speed 35 mph

EXCELSIOR SERIES 61

Although chiefly remembered for his beautiful bicycles, Ignaz Schwinn had his fingers in a number of other pies. In 1907, he founded the Excelsior Motor Manufacturing and Supply Company of Chicago. Recognizing the small step from bicycles to motorcycles, Schwinn produced his first motorcycle, a single-cylinder machine, shortly afterwards.

This model was supplanted by a twin-cylinder, single-speed machine in 1910. The twin continued in production until 1912 when it in turn was replaced by the first of the machines that would eventually make the Excelsior name famous. This was the Series 61, a single-speed, V-twin machine with a capacity of 61 cubic inches (998cc)—hence the "61" designation.

If there was one thing Ignaz Schwinn knew how to do, it was how to dress up a bike, and the Series 61 was an exceptionally beautiful machine. The basic motorcycle was pearl grey, with bright-red panels on the sides of the fuel tank and tool box, and red arrows down the sides of the front forks. These red panels were surrounded by a darker red stripe and then outlined by a gold pinstripe. It all added up to one of the most colorful and attractive machines ever to go on sale on the American market. The model was put on sale in Britain as the American-X,

renamed to distinguish it from the products of the Excelsior company of Coventry, England.

The Series 61 soon proved very popular with the public, the armed forces and police, but in 1915, Ignaz Schwinn went one better. He announced a restyled Series 61, with a gracefully rounded tank and curved top frame—a novelty in an age when most bikes sported the less attractive, angular tanks. The improvements were not confined to restyling, however; the new models also boasted a new and very strong three-speed gearbox.

When America entered World War I in 1917, the 61 went "over there," smartly dressed in olive green with dark-green stripes, and still bearing the famous "X" insignia on its tank.

After the war, Schwinn added the Henderson marque to his stable. In 1920, the Henderson fours and Excelsior twins were launched in a similar paint scheme—a beautiful, deep royal blue with gold striping. In addition, the Excelsior sported new, cushion forks and flashy, white-sidewall balloon tires.

Sales of the Series 61 continued to hold steady, its reputation being further enhanced by some spectacular wins on the mile and half-mile dirt tracks, as well as in many speed and hillclimb

The front leaf-spring suspension on a Series 61 of 1913.

events. For some reason, however, Ignaz Schwinn decided to discontinue production of the Series 61 in 1924, and replace it with a smaller, 45-cubic-inch model known simply as the Super-X.

The new model was neither as popular nor as durable as the old 61 and in 1931, Ignaz Schwinn decided to bring production of both Excelsior and Henderson models to an end. Neither marque was revived, so two famous motorcycling names passed into history.

The single speed, vee-twin engine had a cubic capacity of 61 cubic inches (998cc).

The fine styling of the
Series 61 made it a very
popular machine.

Specification

(1913 model)

engine
Air-cooled, four-stroke, V-twin.
84.1mm (3.31 in.) bore
X 88.9mm (3.50 in.) stroke
= 998.5cc (61 cu.in.). Maximum
power 10 bhp. Compression ratio not
known. Two valves per cylinder,
overhead inlet operated via pushrod
and rocker, side exhaust directly by
one camshaft per cylinder. Single
Schebler carburetor

transmission
Single-speed gearbox.
Chain drive

frame
Single-tube cradle

suspension
Front - Leaf-sprung trailing-link fork
Rear - Solid unsprung

brakes
Front - None
Rear - Drum

performance
Maximum speed 40 mph

HENDERSON FOUR

Of the four-cylinder motorcycles manufactured in the United States during the early part of the 20th Century, the Henderson Fours were perhaps the most successful. During their 19-year lifespan, they also became the world's most famous fours.

It was in 1911 that the Henderson brothers, William G. and Thomas, first announced their intention of going into motorcycle production. A year later they wheeled out the first of their models. The machines were impressive, with in-line, longitudinally mounted four-cylinder engines. The engines featured mechanically operated inlet and exhaust valves, splash lubrication, an enclosed flywheel and Bosch magneto ignition. The Henderson had a clutch but no gearbox and was started by the unusual means of a hand crank at the rear of the engine. Final drive was by chain.

The machine was enormous, with a wheelbase measuring 65 inches. The length allowed room for a pillion seat in front of the rider. William Henderson felt this was the safest position for a passenger. The asking price was $325.

Before long Hendersons were being used to set various endurance records. Carl Clancy of New York became the first man to circle the earth on a motorcycle, his Henderson covering a total of 18,000 miles with no major problems. As a result, the Henderson became very popular with the motorcycling public.

By 1913 the company had made substantial improvements to the forks, frame and tank shape. A year later the first two-speed Henderson appeared, the hand-operated, two-speed gear incorporated in the rear hub. By 1915, the pillion seat had disappeared and the foot board in front of the engine was removed. The machine's wheelbase was also reduced to 59 inches, resulting in considerably improved handling.

The commercial success of the Henderson did not go unnoticed. In 1917, Ignaz Schwinn, head of the Excelsior company, offered to buy out Henderson but allow William and Thomas to remain as executives. The Hendersons sold. Subsequent models appeared with the Excelsior company's

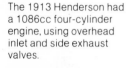

The 1913 Henderson had a 1086cc four-cylinder engine, using overhead inlet and side exhaust valves.

large, red "X" on their tanks.

By 1919, the original Henderson Four models had been phased out and replaced by the new Model K, designed by Arthur Lemon. The Model K had a new, larger (1300cc) engine, and was the first motorcycle to use full-pressure lubrication. The cylinders were of a new type, with inlet and exhaust valves placed side by side, and the drive chain was now fully enclosed. These modifications ensured the new Henderson's popularity.

By this time, however, the Henderson brothers had become thoroughly frustrated in their new roles within the Schwinn organization and they left.

Thomas went into the export business, but William set about establishing a new motorcycle manufacturing concern. Soon afterwards he produced another classic—the Ace Four.

The Excelsior-Henderson company continued production of the Model K until 1922, when it was superseded by the improved De Luxe model. The De Luxe model was the most refined Henderson model up to that date, and it ensured the Henderson name would continue to grow and prosper.

In 1928 came an even better Henderson, the Model KJ. The KJ, designed by Arthur Constantine, was a handsome beast. The familiar four-cylinder

In production terms; the Henderson was far and away the most successful of the early fours.

Instruments and controls on a 1925 De Luxe four-cylinder Henderson.

engine now had five main bearings and enclosed valve gear. Constantine had also returned to the original, overhead-inlet/side-exhaust-valve layout. Very soon the KJ was heralded as the finest four-cylinder motorcycle ever made. The engine produced 40 bhp at 4000 rpm, giving the machine a top speed of 100 mph accompanied by a super smooth ride. An even more powerful version, the KL, was also produced, but was intended mainly for police work.

Production of the KJ and KL models continued until 1931. That year, following a business trip to Washington, Ignaz Schwinn walked into his office and announced, "Gentleman—today we stop." Sch-

winn had realized that the worldwide depression of the 1930s would have devasting effects on the American economy and decided to quit while he was ahead.

The power unit behind the 1925 De Luxe model.

Specification

(1928 model)

engine
Air-cooled, four-stroke, four-cylinder. 68.3mm (2.69 in.) bore X 89mm (3.50 in.) stroke = 1304cc (80 cu.in.). Maximum power 40 bhp at 4000 rpm. Compression ratio not known. Two valves per cylinder, overhead inlet operated by pushrod and rocker and side exhaust operated directly by side camshaft. Single Zenith carburetor.

transmission
Three-speed-and-reverse gearbox. Chain drive

frame
Duplex cradle

suspension
Front - Trailing-link fork
Rear - Solid unsprung

brakes
Front - Drum Rear - Drum

weight
440 lbs. (200kg)

performance
Maximum speed 100 mph

INDIAN BIG CHIEF

While European motorcycle manufacturers have traditionally gone after increased performance through such means as higher compression, higher engine speeds, or more carburetors, Americans have consistently followed the adage, "there's no substitute for cubic inches." It's a philosophy not always shared by the rest of the world, but it does explain the size of the typical American motorcycle, particularly of the 1920s and '30s.

Although a 74-cubic-inch engine was available after 1920, strictly speaking the 74-cubic-inch (1213cc) Indian Big Chief existed from 1923 to 1928 only.

The emergence of the Big Chief as a model in its own right came about because Indian dealers were clamoring for still more speed, power and stamina.

Dublin-born chief engineer Charles B. Franklin set to work to give them what they wanted. Instead of simply boring-out the 61-cubic-inch Chief engine to provide the extra capacity, he enlarged the bore 1/8 inch and lengthened the stroke nearly 1/2 inch. The outcome was a side-valve engine with a loping stride and a top speed near 90 mph.

The performance improved again in 1927. Detachable cylinder heads were fitted, with combustion chambers designed by Harry Ricardo. Later, the Big Chief was given 3.85 x 18-inch low-pressure balloon tires for a more comfortable ride, and restyled handlebars for a more relaxed riding position.

From the first, the Big Chief was equipped with helical-tooth primary gears and an integral three-speed gearbox. The Splitdorf magneto was gear-driven. And while European motorcycles still used the archaic lever throttle, Indians, since 1904, controlled the carburetor by a twistgrip.

When introduced, the machine weighed a hefty 425 lbs., and as time went by it was to grow even heavier. Another point in its disfavor was that, like many machines of the time, Indian fitted a rear brake only.

Not until 1929 did Indian add a front brake, but when that season's models were revealed it was seen that—in name at least—the Big Chief was no more. In truth it was the 61-cubic-inch twin that had been phased out, but the Chief name had been transferred to the bigger machine.

In addition to the standard two-wheeled line, around 1928 the factory was experimenting with a light car carrying very English-looking bodywork. Under the hood, however, was the familiar, 74-cubic-inch Big Chief engine with a chain-driven differential.

That was the way it was to be on into the '30s when, for a time, the big solo was joined by a Chief-engined three-wheeled delivery van. In the final years of producion at the Springfield, Massachusetts, plant, the 74-cubic-inch twin adopted deep-flared fenders and plunger-type rear suspension, but by 1950 it had died.

An Indian Big Chief with a Princess sidecar. This was an ideal machine for those who wanted ample power and seating accomodation to take the family on a day out.

Specification

(1923 model)

engine
Air-cooled, four-stroke, V-twin.
83mm (3.25 in.) bore
X 113mm (4.45 in.) stroke
= 1213cc (74 cu.in.).
Maximum power 24 bhp at
3000 rpm. Two side valves per
cylinder operated via rockers
and pushrods by two
camshafts. Single 1-1/4-in.
Schebler carburetor

transmission
Three-speed gearbox. Chain
drive

frame
Single-down-tube cradle
brakes
Front - None
Rear - Drum
suspension
Front - Leaf-sprung, trailing-
link fork
Rear - Solid unsprung
weight
425 lbs. (193kg)
performance
Maximum speed 90 mph

ACE FOUR

Motorcycling legends are usually created by equal parts of performance, nostalgia and exaggeration. The Ace Four, however, was a machine that needed only the first ingredient. Although its production life only spanned six years—rather stormy years at that—its performance ensured its place in history.

William G. Henderson, also responsible for the Henderson Fours, was the man who created the Ace Four. When the Excelsior company took over Henderson in 1917, William G. became disillusioned with his new role within Excelsior-Henderson and by 1919 had resigned to set up his own company.

His new masterpiece, the Ace Four, made its debut in 1920. Finished in an eye-catching blue with a large, golden eagle painted on the tank, it was the most glamorous machine America had ever seen. The engine was an in-line, 1229cc four cylinder featuring overhead inlet and side exhaust valves—the same arrangement found on the original Hendersons. The lower end included a three-main-bearing crankshaft and splash-fed connecting-rod journals.

Perhaps the most remarkable thing about the Ace, however, was that its weight had been pared down to 365 lbs. (a modern Honda Hawk weighs about 375 lbs.), giving excellent handling and maneuverability.

Right from the start the Ace captured the public's imagination. Ironically, sales were so good that the company nearly collapsed. Seriously undercapitalized, the company simply could not meet its shipments and within a year was in serious financial

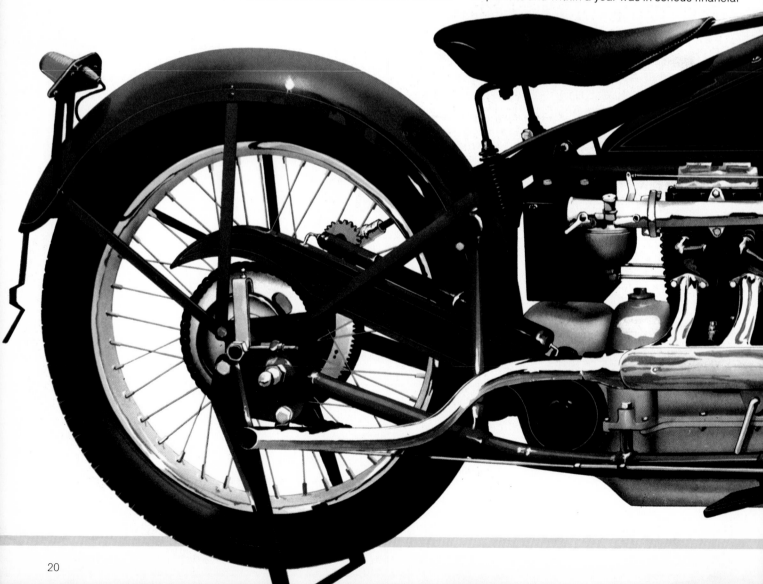

trouble. Fortunately the president, Max Sladkin, managed to find the half-million dollars needed to save the Ace name, but this was only the first of a series of close scrapes for Ace.

By 1922, the Ace Four was setting records of all kinds. In September, Cannonball Baker set a new record for the Los Angeles-to-New York run. Henderson responded in October when Wells Bennett promptly lopped nearly 8 hours off the Baker/Ace record, but the competition helped Ace considerably. The Ace soon became a household name among motorcycling enthusiasts.

That year also saw a prototype of an even more exciting model. This was the Sporting Solo, which featured bigger valves, lightweight connecting rods,

high-compression, light-alloy pistons and a guaranteed top speed of 85 mph.

In October of 1922, William G. Henderson was killed in an accident while testing one of the new season's models. This disaster, however, was overcome when Henderson's former protégé, Arthur O. Lemon, was lured from Excelsior-Henderson to Ace. Lemon had been responsible for the much vaunted Henderson De Luxe model, and in 1924 he produced an improved version of the already impressive Ace Four.

Towards the end of 1923, Ace scored another success when Red Wolverton rode a modified Ace Four through an electronic speed trap at 129 mph, a new world record. The machine Wolverton rode had

Finished in dazzling blue with a large golden eagle decorating the tank, the Ace Four had to be one of the best-looking bikes in its time.

every bit of excess weight trimmed off. The Schebler carburetor was made entirely of aluminium, the pistons, rods and timing gears were extensively lightened and the motor produced 45 bhp at 5400 rpm. The fortunes of Ace had never seemed brighter.

Somewhere along the line, however, the Ace management had been making some serious financial mistakes. Incredibly, the Ace was simply being sold at too low a price. Once again the company was in trouble and before 1924 was out, production of the Ace came to a standsill. The bike was not totally dead, however. In 1926 the Michigan Motor Corporation undertook a rescue operation and a few hundred more Aces were built. Then, in 1927, the assets of the Ace concern passed into the hands of the Indian Motorcycle Company.

The bike was back in production in 1927 as the "Indian Ace." The people at Indian knew a good thing when they saw it, and obtained the talents of Arthur Lemon along with the machine. After a year they changed the name to Indian Four.

Indian continued to produce a four-cylinder model until America entered World War II in 1941. By this time, however, Arthur Lemon was gone and the Ace name forgotten—except by those who had owned one.

Red Wolverton astride his record-breaking Ace Four, being congratulated by designer Arthur Lemon.

right The four-cylinder, four-stroke, air-cooled engine of a 1924 Ace.

A superbly kept example of a 1924 Ace. This particular bike is in the Harrah Museum in Reno, Nevada.

Specification

(1923 model)

engine
Air-cooled, four-stroke, four-cylinder. 69.9mm (2.75 in.) bore X 82.6mm (3.25 in.) stroke = 1266cc (77 cu.in.). Maximum power 20 bhp. Two valves per cylinder, overhead inlet operated by pushrod and rocker and side exhaust operated directly by side camshaft. Single Schebler carburetor

transmission
Three-speed gearbox. Chain drive

frame
Single-down-tube cradle

suspension
Front - Leading-link fork
Rear - Solid unsprung

brakes
Front - None
Rear - Drum, operated by pedal at each side

weight
395 lbs. (179kg)

performance
Maximum speed — 100 mph

CLEVELAND FOUR

In the early '20s, the Cleveland Motorcycle Company of Cleveland, Ohio, was best known for a light-weight single-cylinder machine that proved very popular with American buyers. But by the mid '20s, the success of the Henderson and Ace fours persuaded Cleveland to enter the four-cylinder market.

By late 1925, the first Cleveland four was in production. The design was the work of Detroit engineer L.E. Fowler. The engine of the new Cleveland had a 37-cubic-inch (600cc) displacement, dry-sump lubrication and three-bearing crankshaft. The combustion chamber was T-shaped, much like the Pierce Four of earlier days. The original design had specified shaft drive, but production difficulties arose and a switch was made to chain drive.

Unfortunately, the performance and handling of the new Cleveland left something to be desired, and the company found itself with a flop on its hands. Production ceased after only a few hundred models had been made.

Despite the disappointment, Cleveland remained undaunted, and by 1926 another new four saw the light of day. It was designed by Everitt DeLong, who learned his trade at the elbow of Arthur Lemon of Henderson and Ace fame. The new bike was known as the 4-45 because of its 45-cubic-inch engine. It had an inlet-over-exhaust-valve layout and a single, or monoblock, casting containing all four cylinders. This bike proved a big hit with the public and sales soon began to pick up. Cleveland salesmen were nevertheless aware that they were in a tough market, their 45-cubic-inch model having to compete against the Hendersons and Aces, both sporting engines close to the 80-cubic-inch mark.

In August of 1927, yet another new Cleveland four was announced. Based on the 4-45, the new model was called a 4-61, 61 cubic inches being a more familiar displacement, featuring a 60-cubic-inch (984cc) motor. The familiar F-head valve arrangement was used and a front brake was fitted, making the Cleveland one of the first American machines to be so equipped. This model also pioneered the use of a side stand. The 4-61's top speed was around 90 mph, not far short of the 80-cubic-inch Henderson's.

The 4-61 proved a great success for Cleveland, and in 1929 the concern offered an improved version. This model was known as the Tornado, and it was a handsome beast indeed. A new frame had been designed and a new tank shape created. The engine was fitted with lighter pistons, larger valves and had a higher compression ratio. The Tornado's claimed top speed was in the region of 100 mph, an amazing figure for the times.

Unfortunately, 1929 saw the beginning of the Depression and the Cleveland directors were faced with serious financial problems. Nevertheless, they decided to persevere with the 1930 line, the high point of which was yet another Cleveland 4-61 variation, the now famous Century model. The Century had an even higher compression ratio, polished and enlarged ports, a special exhaust system and a new triple-spring front fork. The Century model was so named because it was a genuine 100 mph machine. Indeed, each one was fitted with a small brass plate on the valve cover proclaiming that it had been personally tested by a Cleveland test rider at a speed in excess of 100 mph.

Only a handful of Century models was ever made. By 1930 the financial climate in America was so severe that Cleveland was finally forced to admit defeat and close is doors, never to reopen.

Specification

(1930 model)

engine
Air-cooled, four-stroke, four-cylinder. 63.5mm (2.50 in.) bore X 72.7mm (3.06 in.) = 984cc (60 cu.in.). Maximum power not known. Compression ratio not known. Two valves per cylinder, overhead inlet operated by pushrod and rocker and side exhaust operated directly from single camshaft. Single Schebler carburetor

transmission
Three-speed gearbox. Chain drive

frame
Duplex cradle

suspension
Front - Leading-link fork
Rear - Solid unsprung
brakes
Front - Drum
Rear - Drum
performance
Maximum speed 100 mph

The 1929 Cleveland sported front and rear brakes, unusual for an American bike of the time.

BROUGH SUPERIOR

Although originally applied to the less exclusive SS80, the Brough Superior SS100 was often hailed as the "Rolls-Royce of motorcycles." After members of the staff at Rolls Royce visited the factory, they conceded that the machine lived up to the title. What George Brough conveniently failed to mention, however, was that the model they inspected was one being set up for show, and its finish was far above the standard.

The SS100's performance, however, was quite different from that of the luxurious car. While the Rolls-Royce was noted more for its grace than performance, in 1925 the Brough could maintain a genuine 100 mph—a speed thought to be beyond the limits of road bikes of its time.

Although Brough Superiors were available with a number of power plants, the first SS100s used a 980cc, 50° V-twin built by J.A. Prestwich especially for Brough. What was most interesting about the engine was its valve gear, which featured four individual camshafts actuating the overhead valves through pushrods. Power output was a claimed 45 bhp at 4500 rpm, with an abundant supply of torque. Carburetion was customer preference, usually by a Wex, B&B or Binks unit, mounted on a T-shaped manifold between the V. Sports models could be had with twin Amal carburetors with long upright inlets.

A four-plate clutch and three-speed Sturmey-Archer gearbox were employed, the ratios giving speeds of 30, 65 and 100 mph. Fuel consumption of the bike could drop to as little as 40 mpg if ridden flat out, but a touring figure of 50 to 55 mpg was obtainable by riders who were content to let the SS100 purr along on a hint of throttle.

Early SS100s used a dual-link front fork modeled after Harley-Davidson's. Detail changes were made and they were patented as "Castle" forks. The fork design was considered by George Brough as ideal for a high-speed bike, but it also meant that an effective, vigorously applied front brake would lock the forks in the fully extended position. This problem never arose, simply because the internal-expanding brake actually fitted was essentially useless. On the other hand, the 8-inch rear brake was extremely effective and care was needed not to lock it up.

With good ground clearance and a weight of 340 lbs., one might think the SS100 was ideal for country-lane riding, but the ponderously heavy steering and long wheelbase meant it was better suited to high-speed road work. Heavy steering hampered town riding, but that was more than made up for by the lusty engine. It made light work of pottering along at low speeds in top gear.

Most of the Broughs were very well equipped, with small windshields, rigid saddle bags (built exclusively for Brough by Brookes), Bonniksen time-and-distance speedometers and an immaculate finish, topped off by a nickel-plated fuel tank.

In 1933, the SS100 was redesigned with a 988cc, JAP engine, a four-speed gearbox and minor alterations. Two years later a Matchless power unit was installed. Brough was not averse to changing suppliers if he felt he could improve the machine, or the quality was being compromised.

Much of the SS100's fame was due to the showman in George Brough, for the numbers could never justify it. Less than 3000 Brough Superiors were ever manufactured, and fewer than 500 SS100s. Production ceased at the start of World War II.

below & right The engine of the Le Vac, Ron Storey works sprinter of 1927.

Specification

(1933 model)

engine
Air-cooled, four-stroke, JAP V-twin.
85.5mm (3.36 in.) bore
X 86mm (3.38 in.) stroke
= 988cc (60.26 cu.in.) Maximum
power 45 bhp at 4500 rpm.
Compression ratio not known. Two
valves per cylinder, operated via
pushrods and rockers by four
individual camshafts. Single
carburetor, customer choice

transmission
Three-speed gearbox. Chain drive

frame
Single-tube cradle

suspension
Front - Castle leading-link, friction-
damper fork
Rear - Solid unsprung

brakes
Front - Drum
Rear - Drum

weight
340 lbs. (154kg)

performance
Maximum speed 100 mph
Fuel consumption approximately
45 mpg

One of the many achievements of this 1927
Brough Superior SS100 was to beat Sir Malcolm
Campbell's supercharged Sunbeam at the
Brighton speed trials in 1932.

COVENTRY EAGLE

Although the Brough Superior is probably the most famous high-performance English machine from the '20s and '30s, it was certainly not the only one. A number of manufacturers, including AJS, MacEvoy, Conventry-B&D, Grindlay Peerless, and Croft Cameron specialized in the high-performance market. Most of these models were, like the Brough, powered by large, V-twin engines by J.A. Prestwich, Matchless or AMC, and many looked quite similar. And much to George Brough's chagrin, one of them, the Coventry Eagle, often matched the Brough's performance.

It would be a mistake, however, to discount the Coventry Eagle Flying Eight as just a slavish copy. It was more a case of "great minds think alike." George Brough and Percy Mayo were student friends who, as World War I came to a close, would often talk far into the night about the dream bikes that each would build once peace came again.

Mayo unveiled his masterpiece in late 1922. It was, said the trade press, "...particularly handsome and symmetrical. As a fast touring machine, the new 976cc twin suggests unlimited possibilities." They commented also that the finish was of the very finest—and so it was, with the bullnosed saddle tank decked out in black and carmine red.

The engine was the JAP side-valve Super Sports, and though the new bike had no model name when first announced, it soon gained the title "Flying Eight." The "eight" was a reference to its nominal 8hp classification—not its power output, of course,

but assessed from a Royal Automobile Club formula based on piston diameter.

From the start, it had all-chain drive and a three-speed Sturmey-Archer gearbox. Despite the daunting price of £145 (a comparable BSA V-twin was about £70) it attracted a discerning clientele.

For 1924, the model underwent a complete redesign, adopting Best and Lloyd mechanical lubrication, balloon tires, large-diameter ball races in the steering head, and a much heavier frame in which the lower tank rails and rear sub-frame tubes were duplicated. Also, a very big step forward, Lucas Magdyno electric lighting was standardized.

There were even better things to come from Coventry Eagle. They enlisted the aid of Brooklands racing star Bert LeVack. LeVack's track experience led to the development of a whole family of Flying Eights for the 1925 season, all making use of a lighter, yet stronger frame. Other details included a Webb center-spring front fork, 8-inch-diameter Royal Enfield brakes and, on the top-of-the-range model, a Jardine gearbox.

That top model employed for the first time an overhead-valve 976cc twin. This was the same JAP power unit found in the new Brough Superior SS100. There was a standard two-cam side-valve at £120, a four-cam side-valve (another new JAP motor, also powering the Brough SS80) at £135, and the overhead-valve job at £165. In each instance these prices were just £5 under those of the equivalent Brough Superior.

Apart from cosmetic changes, a more handsome headlamp, a better layout of the twin exhaust pipes, and the adoption of "Whispering Ghost" mufflers, there was little further change in the make-up of the Flying Eight. One more version was added in 1927 only, a bargain-priced, two-cam side-valver offered without electric lighting. It could be that this was an attempt to clear the decks, prior to a change of policy by the Mayo family.

That year there had been a significant addition to the Coventry Eagle line in the form of a Villiers-powered two-stroke in a new stamped-steel frame. The last Flying Eights were cataloged for 1929, and by then the teething troubles of the stamped-steel frame had been overcome. The future, reckoned the Mayos, lay not in expensive V-twins, but in cheap commuter models. Time was to prove them right.

Established in Victorian times as cycle makers operating under the Royal Eagle trademark, this Coventry-based company became known as Coventry Eagle early in the 1900s when it started the manufacture of motorcycles.

Specification

(1922 model)

engine
Air-cooled, four-stroke, V-twin.
85.5mm (3.36 in.) bore X 85mm
(3.34 in.) stroke = 976cc (59.60
cu.in.). Maximum power 28 bhp.
Compression ratio 6.5:1. Two valves
per cylinder operated via pushrods
and rockers by a single camshaft.
Single carburetor

transmission
Jardine three-speed gearbox. Chain
drive

frame
Open tubular

suspension
Front - Webb Girder fork
Rear - Solid unsprung

brakes
Front - Drum
Rear - Drum

weight
385 lbs. (175kg)

performance
Maximum speed—100 mph

above & left A 1925
Coventry Eagle. This is a
side-valve model, the
Flying Eight.

SCOTT FLYING SQUIRREL

There are those who declare that the Scott company's long-standing affection for the Squirrel model name was a reflection of the machine's habit of scattering nuts around. Not true, of course, but nevertheless, the Shipley menagerie of Squirrels, Touring Squirrels, Flying Squirrels and Super Squirrels can certainly be confusing to the uninitiated.

Essentially, the Flying Squirrel was the sports-roadster member of the range, new at London's Olympia Show of September, 1925, and destined to have a production life of 25 years. It was, said Scott, a road-going version of the factory's two-stroke, TT-racing model. Although the familiar open frame was retained, an oval fuel tank was clamped to the seat tube. The big TT-type tank, fitting between saddle and steering head, could be supplied at extra cost.

To customer's choice, a 498cc or 596cc engine could be supplied. Compared to the TT engine, the street models featured bigger, polished exhaust ports. A redesigned cylinder head provided more efficient cooling in the region of the spark plugs. Mechanical oiling was handled by a Best and Lloyd pump, mounted on the crankcase door and driven by a peg from the overhung crank.

Listed at £86 in the 498cc size (or £3 more for the 596cc version) the first Flying Squirrel weighed only 240 lbs. A year later a change to a heavier triangulated duplex frame and to a close-ratio, three-speed gearbox and multi-plate clutch helped send the weight up to 315 lbs.

Although a whole host of minor refinements crept in over the years, the basic specifications remained unaltered to the end of production at Shipley in 1950. For a time Scott featured a Flying Squirrel de Luxe, which was actually a whole family of Squirrels varying in degree of tune or trim.

The Scott was one of these machines that a rider either loved or hated; it was an acquired taste. Production was never very high and there were occasions when the manufacturers were in very deep waters financially.

Not surprisingly, two-stroke development at the time of the Flying Squirrel's heyday was nothing like the exact science it is today. The bike could manage a top speed of 75—80 mph in production trim, but that was a compromise with reasonable fuel economy. Certainly the Flying Squirrel would respond to tuning if its owner had no objection to the loss of reliability and the higher fuel bills that inevitably resulted.

Scotts were road-raced, but usually the models chosen were the TT Replica or Sprint Special, rather than the Flying Squirrel. In 1927, however, J. Shuckburgh Wright equipped a Flying Squirrel with a supercharger, intending to compete at Brooklands. Alas, it was wasted effort. The Brooklands track is situated in a heavily built-up area and machines competing at the track must be fitted with a muffler. Even with the huge, lozenge-shaped "Brooklands cans" in place, the noise from the blown Squirrel caused the race officials to bar him from practice after only one lap.

After a World War II close-down, the Flying Squirrel returned in late 1948, at first with Webb girder forks, but soon with Dowty telescopic air forks. Only the 596cc model was offered, however, and after two years the Shipley works had closed.

Limited production restarted in Birmingham a few years later—but only of the Clubman Special, basically a 1939 model. Although production of spare parts continues through a number of devotees, 1950 was the year of the Squirrel's last flight.

below The badge of the Scott motorcycle, named after its inventor Alfred Angas Scott.

opposite top A superb example of the 1930 498cc Flying Squirrel.

opposite bottom The single carburetor used on the above model.

Specification

(1926 model)

engine
Water-cooled, two-stroke, twin-cylinder. 74.6mm (2.93 in.) bore X 68.25mm (2.68 in.) stroke = 596cc (36 cu.in.). Maximum power 28 bhp at 5000 rpm. Compression ratio not known. Single Amal carburetor

transmission
Two-speed gearbox. Chain drive

frame
Open, semi-triangulated tubular

suspension
Front - Scott telescopic fork
Rear - Solid unsprung

brakes
Front - Drum
Rear - Drum

weight
327 lbs. (148kg)

performance
Maximum speed 75 mph
Fuel consumption approximately 45 mpg

MATCHLESS SILVER HAWK

At the London Show in the autumn of 1930, two new exciting and attractive machines were unveiled to the British public. Both were four-cylinder models. In time, both would come to be regarded as classics.

The two machines were the Ariel Square Four and the Matchless Silver Hawk. During the next quarter of a century the Ariel attracted a loyal following while the Matchless fizzled after five years.

The arrival of the Matchless was not wholly unexpected by enthusiasts. A year earlier, the Collier brothers of London had attracted much attention with the Silver Arrow, a machine with a 400cc, narrow-angle V-twin. So the Colliers followed it up with a 591cc model, though with four cylinders set in V-formation and using an overhead-camshaft arrangement instead of the Silver Arrow's side valves.

Enthusiasts of the Matchless marque were quick to spot the similarities between the Silver Arrow and the larger Hawk. Both engines had an included cylinder angle of 26°, but in the Hawk they were arranged in double-V formation in one block with air spaces around the barrels. A two-throw crankshaft was supported on three main bearings—plain phosphor-bronze journals on the ends and rollers in the center. The enclosed cam gear was carried within the one-piece head and shaft-driven from the right side. The shaft also drove the generator/distributor unit through a bevel gear at its base.

Outwardly the two Matchless models were also similar. In laying out the Hawk, the Colliers retained a number of Arrow features, such as the pivoted, triangulated rear suspension, front-mounted oil tank and an instrument panel atop the handlebars. Another Arrow feature carried over was the braking system, where the foot pedal worked both the front and rear drums. At the time of its introduction, the Silver Hawk was the only rear-sprung four-cylinder machine in production.

below In 1930 Matchless launched their revolutionary Silver Hawk model.

The exact power output of the Hawk's V-four engine was not disclosed, but a compression ratio of 6.1:1 and an overall weight of around 380 lbs. gave the machine a top speed of approximately 85 mph, while fuel consumption of 75—80 mpg could be expected.

In spite of its technical innovations, the Silver Hawk was not a great sales success for Matchless. The initial reason was the model's price—£75—at a time when the world was suffering from a huge depression. Motorcyclists were simply not prepared to pay for innovation when similar performance was available at lower cost. Secondly, although the engine in the Silver Hawk was exceptionally smooth, the single cylinder head tended to overheat when the bike was really ridden hard.

By the end of 1935, both the Silver Arrow and Silver Hawk were things of the past. Only 500—550 Silver Hawks were ever produced. Today the Silver Hawk is a recognized classic, but in its day it was simply too much motorcycle at too high a price.

Specification

(1930 model)

engine
Air-cooled, four-stroke, V-four.
50.8mm (2.0 in.) bore
X 73mm (2.87 in.) stroke
= 591cc (36 cu.in.). Maximum power approximately 26 bhp. Compression ratio 6.1:1. Two valves per cylinder operated via rockers by a single overhead camshaft. Single SU carburetor

transmission
Four-speed gearbox. Chain drive

frame
Single-down-tube cradle

suspension
Front - Friction-damped fork
Rear - Triangulated sprung unit

brakes
Front - Drum
Rear - Drum

weight
380 lbs. (172kg)

performance
Maximum speed 85 mph
Fuel consumption approximately 75 mpg

right   This example of the Silver Hawk engine is now kept in the Science Museum, London.

ARIEL SQUARE FOUR

It is an oft-told part of motorcycling folklore that London-born Edward Turner sketched out his idea for an entirely new type of four-cylinder engine (with the cylinders arranged like the four dots on dice) on the inside of a cigarette packet, took a train to the midlands and hawked the scheme all around the British motorcycle industry.

The people at AJS were tempted, but turned it down after second thought. Yet there was a good fairy waiting in the wings after all, in the form of Jack Sangster, chief of the Ariel factory. He gave Edward Turner his chance, and the outcome was a machine that took the 1930 London Olympia Show by storm. The same exhibition saw the coming of a rival four-cylinder machine, a narrow-angle monobloc design from London's Matchless factory, known as the Silver Hawk. Good as the Silver Hawk may have been, however, it was destined to live in the shadow of the Ariel Square Four.

Turner's new Square Four engine was, in effect, a pair of vertical twins with all four cylinders in a single casting and their crankshafts coupled by central spur gears. The crankshafts were built-up pieces, with three of the crank throws overhung, or single-sided. The fourth was a full crank, with an output shaft providing the primary drive to the gearbox. Originally Turner had planned a unit-construction engine, light enough to be fitted into the stan-

below An advertisement for the Ariel Square Four of 1937.

right Edward Turner's remarkable Square Four of 1931.

The
SQUARE FOUR
1000 c.c. MODEL 4C £90
600 c.c. MODEL 4F £84

dard Ariel 250cc frame. For policy reasons—the Ariel works had a contract with Burman, the gearbox manufacturer—a separate engine and gearbox were used for the production versions.

The first Square Four was a 500cc model with a single, chain-driven overhead camshaft, but before long the capacity had been raised to 600cc, and the smaller model dropped after a couple of years.

Inevitably, the new machine attracted the attention of those who wanted to make it go a whole lot faster than the makers had intended, and these included Cambridge University clubman Howard Somerville Sikes, and Brooklands speed specialist Ben Bickell. Both had the idea of building supercharged 500cc Square Fours, but each for different reasons. Sikes wanted his for the 1931 Senior TT, while Bickell had the aim of covering 100 miles in an hour.

Unhappily, both men were thwarted—for the same reason. Under stress, the head tended to overheat, blowing the head gasket in the process. Nevertheless, in the course of an endurance test for which the Ariel company gained the coveted Maude's Trophy, a 500cc Square Four did succeed, under ACU observation, in packing 700 miles into 700 minutes.

In the late '30s the Square Four underwent a complete redesign, emerging as a 997cc model. Gone was the overhead camshaft, the front-mounted carburetor, the horizontally split crankcase and the built-up crankshafts.

This was the model for which the claim of "ten to a hundred in top gear" was made. Indeed, the sheer effortlessness of the Ariel's power delivery was its greatest charm. But as time passed, each refinement—such as the compensated-link rear suspension—added just a little more weight.

The model was given a weight reduction in 1949 via an aluminum-alloy cylinder block and head. This not only cut the weight of the machine, but improved the cooling considerably. Four years later the machine was given a four-pipe head and higher compression, and redubbed the Mark II. Never a model of efficient breathing, the improvements in head design finally gave the machine performance befitting a 1000cc machine. The Ariel Square Four did not die until 1958, and in the eyes of many enthusiasts the last were the best of all.

above The 1000cc Square Four of 1951.

opposite The redesigned Square Four engine of 1954.

Specification

(1949 model)

engine
Air-cooled, four-stroke, four-cylinder. 65mm (2.56 in.) bore X 75mm (2.95 in.) stroke = 997cc (61 cu.in.). Maximum power 34.5 bhp at 5500 rpm. Compression ratio 6:1. Two valves per cylinder operated via pushrods and rockers by a single central camshaft. Single SU carburetor

transmission
Four-speed gearbox. Chain drive

frame
Single-down-tube cradle

suspension
Front - Telescopic fork
Rear - Plunger-link sprung

brakes
Front - Drum
Rear - Drum

weight
430 lbs. (195kg)

performance
Maximum speed 98 mph
Fuel consumption approximately 42 mpg

ZÜNDAPP K800

A casual vistor to the Berlin Motor Cycle Show in February, 1933 may have stopped dead in his tracks at the Zündapp stand. The effects of the Great Depression were still being felt throughout the motorcycle industries of the world. Many factories had gone under; others were merely ticking over with very restricted programs. Yet Zündapp, at who knows what cost, had thrown its range of small two-strokes overboard for a totally new line-up, each using a stamped-steel frame.

There were still two small two-strokes, but the remaining models consisted of a transverse, 500cc side-valve flat twin and, more significant, the K600 and K800 side-valve flat fours. The significance of the "K" prefix was that the four-strokes were equipped with *Kardan*, or shaft final drive.

Although a stamped-steel frame can be produced more rapidly and cheaply than an equivalent tubular frame, the necessary tooling is expensive. The cost can only be justified if long-term, high-volume production is expected. Although designer Richard Xavier Kuechen had spread the cost by using the same frame for the three larger models, the firm still seemed to be taking a big gamble. In addition to the expense, the exposed flat plates which formed the major structure of the frame made the machines look somewhat bulky and unfinished.

On the other hand, the K600 and K800 engines were compact and well integrated. Each pair of

cylinders was cast as a monobloc, and the engines were characterized by a number of beautifully smooth, light-alloy castings. The engines featured a one-piece crankshaft with plain bearings for the rods and mains, and a heavy flywheel/clutch at the rear. At the front of the engine, a short chain ran up to the camshaft. A louvred cover over the engine enclosed the generator, single carburetor, coil and distributor.

The transverse, 791cc *Doppleboxermotor* of the K800 was direct-coupled to the four-speed transmission, but the shaft final drive certainly didn't mean that chains weren't used. On the contrary, the "gearbox" contained no gears at all, but four dual-row chains. Sprockets on the input and output shafts provided different ratios, with drives selected by dog clutches.

Power output of the K800 was said to be 22 bhp, modest by today's standards but fairly impressive in 1933. Impressive, too, was its performance in the hills of North Wales, site of the 1933 International Six Days Trial held in September. Showing great faith in their new product, Zündapp entered a factory team comprising J. von Krohn, P. Butow and O. Baylon. One of the toughest climbs of the trial was at Dinas Rock which, said a contemporary report, "...the Zündapp of von Krohn climbed without a whisper."

All three machines finished the event, von Krohn with no points lost and a gold medal. Somewhat less skilled, Butow and Baylon had to be content with bronze medals.

Although the K600 was dropped in 1934, few changes were made in the K800. The cast, light-alloy footboards at each side were redesigned to swing down as propstands. Throughout the '30s the big flat-four developed a small but loyal following, who nicknamed it "the green elephant."

During the late '30s, Zündapp added several more powerful overhead-valve twins and development on the K800 shifted to military applications. But as the war approached, the K800 was dropped so the factory could concentrate on a more modern overhead-valve twin, the KS750.

During this time, Zündapp stepped up production to meet military needs, and this was where the changeover to a stamped-steel frame paid off. The K800's frame lived on with the KS750 twin, which, with a driven sidecar, was to become familiar in every field of battle in which the Wehrmacht was engaged.

right Rear view of the Zündapp K800, with its easily detachable saddlebags.

opposite Front suspension layout of the K800.

The K800 in military guise.

Specification

(1933 model)

engine
Air-cooled, four-stroke, flat four-cylinder. 62mm (2.44 in.) bore X 66mm (2.59 in.) stroke = 791cc (48 cu.in.). Maximum power 22 bhp at 4300 rpm. Compression ratio 5.8:1. Two side valves per cylinder operated directly by a single central camshaft. Single 30mm Pallas/Amal carburetor

transmission
Four-speed gearbox. Shaft drive

frame
Stamped-steel cradle

suspension
Front - Girder fork with hydraulic damping
Rear - Solid unsprung

brakes
Front - Drum
Rear - Drum

weight
415 lbs. (188kg)

performance
Maximum speed 80 mph
Fuel consumption approximately 55 mpg

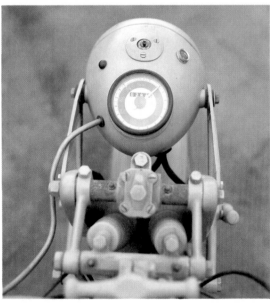

far left The dynamo and carburetor top housing removed.

left The headlamp unit.

BSA GOLD STAR

The story of the BSA Gold Star goes back to 1937 when the company introduced a new 500cc single-cylinder model called the Empire Star. At that time, a gold star was awarded at the Brooklands circuit to any rider who managed to lap at over 100 mph during a race. Although BSA had not entered into competition since 1921 the staff wondered if their new sporty single could be tuned up to win one of the prizes. Jack Amott and Len Crisp decided to try, and persuaded Wal Handley to come out of retirement for the attempt.

On June 30, 1937 the scene was set. Handley was entered in a three-lap outer-circuit event. By the second lap he had fought his way to the front of the field, finally finishing several hundred yards ahead. His average speed was 102.27 mph, with one amazing lap of 107.57 mph! At the Earls Court Show the following year, a replica of that famous machine was shown and, not surprisingly, it was called the Gold Star.

The Gold Star received the model number M24, but the production model was certainly quite different from Handley's mount. The cylinder head and barrel on the production model were aluminum, with an austenitic-iron liner and valve-seat inserts. The valve gear was enclosed and lubricated by a pressure-feed, dry-sump system with the oil tank beneath the saddle. Drive to the rear wheel was by chain, a four-speed Elektron gearbox and a multi-plate clutch. Fuel/air mixture was provided by an Amal TT carburetor.

Each power unit fitted neatly into a triangular-cradle frame was made from high-tensile-strength steel tubing. At the front were Webb-type girder forks with an adjustable friction damper, while the

The 1938 BSA Gold Star.

rear end remained solid. Brakes consisted of 7-in. X 1-3/8-in. drums at both front and rear with smooth but powerful action. From 30 mph the stopping distance was 28 feet, a figure well on par with even its modern counterparts.

Although the Gold Star legend speaks highly of the machine's high-speed prowess, high speeds on the original Gold Stars tended to bring out gremlins in the rigid frame. It was not until the machine was updated with telescopic forks and some semblance of rear suspension that the "Goldie" could be described as a "good handler."

On paper, starting the big single was easy: "tickle" the carburetor, retard the ignition and "bump" the bike over while in gear to find the compression stroke. Once neutral had again been located, a quick prod on the kickstarter usually—one hoped—brought the beast to life. In the real world, grown men were reduced to pleading, blubbering idiots while attempting the ritual. Under these circumstances, riders were known to create their own meanings for the initials "BSA"—few complimentary, most crude.

Once running, the performance of the Gold Star was commendable. Acceleration was brisk, and a top speed around 90 mph could be achieved. For normal cruising, though, the engine felt best at a speed of around 70 mph. Fuel consumption was generally in the 65-mpg region.

In 1940 the war prevented further production of the big single, so the factory concentrated on its "khaki cousin," the M20. It wasn't until 1948 that the model returned, first as a 350 and later as a 500. In addition, the suspension was vastly improved, with telescopic front forks and plunger rear suspension. Later the design was again revised, this time with a swingarm rear suspension, and the machine came into its full glory.

Light weight, nimble handling and a willing engine gave the bike all the requirements of a fine, grass-roots racer. Many performance parts were offered to transform the basic roadster. In fact, the engine was offered in several stages of tune, depending on the competitive wants of the customer.

In the US, Gold Stars are best remembered for their performances against the Harley-Davidson KRs on AMA dirt tracks. Tuned far beyond any British definition of "reliable," the big thumpers claimed the Ascot track in Los Angeles, California as home.

Specification

(1958 model)

engine
Air-cooled, four-stroke, single-cylinder. 85mm (3.35 in.) bore
X 88mm (3.46 in.) stroke
= 499cc (30 cu.in.). Maximum power
37 bhp at 6800 rpm. Compression
ratio 8.5:1. Two valves per cylinder
operated via pushrods and rockers
by a single camshaft. Single
1-5/32-in. Amal TT carburetor

transmission
Four-speed gearbox. Chain drive

frame
Duplex cradle

suspension
Front - Telescopic forks
Rear - Swingarm with Girling coil-over shocks

brakes
Front - Drum Rear - Drum

weight
3l5 lbs. (l43kg)

performance
Maximum speed 90 mph
Fuel consumption approximately 64 mpg

above & left A 1960
500cc Gold Star. The
machine saw its last year
of production just three
years later.

VINCENT BLACK SHADOW

Although the word "superbike" had not been coined in the days of the Vincent Black Shadow, this superb machine stands today as the epitome of the term. People who know nearly nothing about motorcycles, or the Vincent itself, will acknowledge the name with a quick nod or an approving smile. The brainchild of Philip Vincent and Phil Irving, the big V-twin bike was an outstanding combination of innovative and proven engineering.

The heart of a big bike is the engine, and in the Vincent's case this was particularly true, for it also formed the main chassis member. The crankcase and gearbox were integral, and the steering head and rear suspension bolted to them. Using the engine as a stressed member made a much more flex-free chassis than the then-current single or duplex cradle. Engine bearings were set up in a similar way to distribute crankshaft loads throughout the cases.

In its original Series-A form based on the 500cc HRD single, the Vincent's cylinders had a 47° included angle. The power of the original engine, however, caused all manner of problems with the clutch and transmission. In the course of a complete redesign for the Series-B, Irving increased the angle to 50°. Viewed from the front, the cylinders were offset, front to the right, rear to the left, to allow cooling air to reach the rear cylinder. Cooling was also helped by having the exhaust ports at the front of the cylinders for an unobstructed flow of air.

To minimize valve-train inertia, the side camshafts were mounted quite high up in the engine, and opened the valves through short pushrods and rockers. The valve train was extremely unusual, using forked rockers that engaged the valves by a groove cut midway down the valve stem. Each valve had two guides, one above and one below the rocker, to minimize wear. The long valve stem and the rocker arrangement also allowed the valve springs to be mounted a good distance from the combustion chamber for minimum heat transfer and good cooling.

In Series-C form, the "undersquare" 998cc unit produced 55 bhp at 5700 rpm, a respectable figure, particularly considering the engine's 7.3:1 compression ratio. The engine's torque output was considerable, and even with 458 lbs. of bike to push along, performance was more than adequate. When it was introduced, a Series B model was tested at a speed of 122 mph, while its standing-start quarter-

mile was comfortably under the 15-second mark. Fuel consumption averaged out just under 50 mpg, which is respectable in any company.

As with the engine, detail on the rest of the bike

was rather special, with such niceties as a hinged rear mudguard which offered easy access to the rear wheel. Other touches included front forks which allowed the spring rate and the amount of trail to be altered for sidecar work.

At the rear, a cantilever system pivoted on tapered roller bearings, with two almost horizontal coil-over shocks mounted under the seat. The unusual, all-alloy "Girdraulic" forks combined the rigidity of girder forks with the hydraulic damping of telescopic. Seven-inch brake drums were mounted

A cut-away drawing of the Vincent series B Black Shadow.

on either side of each wheel-hub, so they were well cooled and very powerful. That same road test of the Series B proved the bike could achieve 1.3 g stops, a figure which could probably not be bettered today.

To take some of the effort out of kick-starting, a decompressor valve was fitted—a kick-back from this engine was not to be taken lightly. The Vincent was deceptively quick, as the engine was a powerful "slogger" rather than a high revving unit. The cruising speed depended very much on the rider's stamina, for just about any speed up to maximum could be held for as long as the rider could endure.

The seating position was quite comfortable, although the braker lever was on the left and the "upside-down"—up for first—gearchange on the right, unlike modern-day practice. The grips were quite close together and low mounted, so the rider had to lean forward slightly, but this was a comfortable rather than awkward pose for the open road.

Undoubtedly, the Vincent Black Shadow was a rider's bike, with excellent performance, economy, braking and handling. It was also very well finished and comprehensively equipped. While Phil Vincent and company gave the public that sort of specification, even at a high price, the bike enthusiasts were happy. When he tried to give them a glimpse of the future with the faired Black Knight, however, they lost all interest. By the time the unfaired Series D arrived, it was probably too late.

right A hinged rear mudguard offered easy access to the Vincent rear wheel.

below right Its famous and prominent speedometer.

below far right The engine of the Vincent Series C Black Shadow, with later-model Amal carburetors.

opposite page The tail light (top) and the Vincent HRD emblem on the tank (bottom).

Specification

(1952 model)

engine
Air-cooled, four-stroke, V-twin. 84mm (3.30 in.) bore X 90mm (3.54 in.) stroke = 998cc (61 cu.in.). Maximum power 55 bhp at 5700 rpm. Compression ratio 7.3:1. Two valves per cylinder operated via pushrods and rockers by two central camshafts. Two Amal carburetors

transmission
Four-speed gearbox. Chain drive

frame
Boxed-section backbone using engine as a stressed member

suspension
Front - Girdraulic fork
Rear - Vincent cantilever system

brakes
Front - Dual drum
Rear - Dual drum

weight
458 lbs. (208kg)

performance
Maximum speed 125 mph
Fuel consumption approximately 40 mpg

NORTON DOMINATOR

Revealed at the Earls Court Show of 1948, the Norton Dominator went on to become one of the most successful roadsters available during the '50s and early '60s. The 497cc Dominator was designed by the much respected Bert Hopwood, formerly associated with BSA and Ariel. His latest creation was to set the Norton design trend for many years to come. In fact, even the last model produced by Norton, the 850 Commando, bears a close resemblance to the Dominator.

The original engine was the classic vertical twin with pushrod-operated overhead valves. With a bore and stroke of 66mm X 73mm and a compression ratio of 6.7:1, the Dominator engine was tuned rather mildly, with a top speed in the high eighties.

In 1953 the original plunger rear suspension was replaced by a more efficient swingarm arrangement. Shortly afterwards a 600cc model was added, and the frame changed to the famous "Featherbed"—a legend in itself. Either model had potent response and excellent road manners. The sports-minded enthusiast now could experience the race-bred qualities that had previously been confined to the track.

The 1961 "Sports Special" was typical of the series, despite various modifications over the standard version. Most notable was the absence of a muffler on the left side. Instead, siamese pipes were utilized and these aided ground clearance when enthusiastic riding was called for. In fact, ground clearance was so good that only tire adhesion determined the angles of the lean available.

Handling was also exceptional, and on long, twisting country roads, the Dominator was a joy to ride. With positive steering and taut handling it gave the rider an unsurpassed degree of confidence. Obviously, the "Featherbed" frame was partly responsible, but the suspension was also of a high standard. Norton's own "Roadholder" front forks were used, complemented at the rear by Girling shocks with adjustable springs. The ride obtained was slightly on the firm side, but not uncomfortable.

The 600cc sports version produced 36 bhp at 7000 rpm, a good 6 bhp over the standard unit. This was mainly due to the twin Amal "Monobloc" carburetors, bigger inlet valves and ports. Also, a special camshaft was fitted and the crankshaft strengthened to take the extra output.

Generally, the Dominator had a very good temperament. If starting followed the customary drill, there was no difficulty in starting up a cold motor. After a few kicks the engine would burst into life and the bike would soon be ready to pull away without argument or hesitation.

In town the Dominator was docile and pleasant to use, but once on the open road the bike would change into a beast that quickly swallowed up the miles. Into top gear, and the power would begin to surge once it got to 50 mph. Brisk acceleration would continue right past the magic "ton" until a top speed of around 110 mph was reached. Vibration was always present, but due to the motor's small displacement, never became excessive, even when the motor was red-lined through the gears. Even at 7000 rpm, the motor never felt strained. Gear

right The top of a Norton Dominator headlamp, with the speedometer in the center, ammeter on the right and light switch on the left.

opposite A fine example of a 1959 Norton 88 Dominator. It used a twin-cylinder 497cc engine and the "Featherbed" frame.

changes needed positive use of the clutch, but generally the gearbox never caused concern.

The bike also excelled in braking. An 8-inch drum at the front and a 7-inch at the rear gave surefooted stops. They were surprisingly fade resistant, even under extended, high-speed use. In the wet the units remained fully watertight; only tire adhesion was responsible for the longer stopping distances. In the dry, braking from 30 mph could be done in approximately 27 feet.

Despite some niggling faults the bike was an excellent sports machine. It cried out to be ridden hard and, as a connoisseur's mount, the Dominator performed admirably—a true classic.

Specification

(1961 model)

engine
Air-cooled, four-stroke, twin-cylinder.
68mm (2.7 in.) bore
X 82mm (3.23 in.) stroke
= 597cc (36 cu.in.). Maximum power
36 bhp at 7000 rpm. Compression
ratio 8.5:1. Two valves per cylinder
operated by pushrods and rockers
by a single, rear-mounted camshaft.
Two 1-1/16-in. Amal Monobloc
carburetors
transmission
Four-speed gearbox. Chain drive
frame
Full duplex cradle
suspension
Front - Norton "Roadholder"
telescopic forks
Rear - Swingarm with Girling coil-
over shocks
brakes
Front - Drum
Rear - Drum
weight
408 lbs. (185kg)
performance
Maximum speed 110 mph
Fuel consumption approximately
63 mpg

During the 1950s and early '60s the Dominator became one of the most successful bikes available.

BSA ROCKET III & TRIUMPH TRIDENT

By 1968, the British motorcycle industry was in serious trouble. The Japanese had made such inroads that several UK companies had already gone under. In an attempt to stave off disaster, the BSA and Triumph companies announced their entries into the 750cc market with the nearly identical Triumph Trident and BSA Rocket III. These two so captured the public imagination that a new word was coined for them, "superbike."

The pair also reintroduced several words to the British motorcycling vocabulary—*smooth, fast* and *ugly*. The bikes were a welcome departure from tradition in a number of ways, but the styling was charitably described as "uninspired." Gone was the graceful teardrop tank of the Triumph Bonneville or the sculptured side panels of the BSA Lightning. Instead were flat side panels and breadloaf tanks. The tapered mufflers of both were replaced by stamped-steel units with styling by Buck Rogers.

But they were fast. The claimed output of 60 bhp at 7250 rpm gave the 470-lb. triples a top speed around 120 mph and quarter-mile times under 14 seconds. That made them the fastest production machines available at the time, though this record was exceptionally short-lived.

The most unusual feature of the Rocket and Trident models was their three-cylinder engines, a configuration never widely used in motorcycling.

The engine was fitted with three Amal carburetors and had a compression ratio of 9.5:1. Triple coils and contact points gave tuners fits, while the electrics included the inevitable Lucas alternator. The cylinder block and head were one-piece, light-alloy castings. Valve arrangement was the same Edward Turner used in the original 1937 Triumph Speed Twin—front and rear camshafts operating pushrods enclosed in tubes. An archaic four-speed gearbox was fitted with chain final drive.

The major difference between the two was in the frame. The BSA used a duplex-cradle with its engine inclined forward, while the Triumph had a single-down-tube with the engine upright.

On the road, the two were impressive machines. Handling was up to English standards and braking was adequate, in spite of the fact that a drum brake only was fitted to the front wheel.

The machines were completely restyled the year after their introduction but never sold well. A few months after their introduction, the outrageous, 500cc Kawasaki triple stole their "quickest production" status. Later, the Honda 750 and Kawasaki Z-1, with their superior performance and sophistication pushed the Rocket III and Trident into the category of "also-ran."

With the formation of Norton Villiers Triumph in 1972, the BSA name died, and with it the Rocket III. Triumph continued the Trident, adding disc brakes, electric start and a five-speed gearbox. A long-rumored 900cc version never materialized, and in time the Trident ceased production. With it went Britain's last foothold.

right Two views of the Triumph Trident engine. The oil cooler is positioned above the exhaust pipes and just behind the front downtube.

opposite page Two very different Tridents. The above is a mid-1970s model and below the original version.

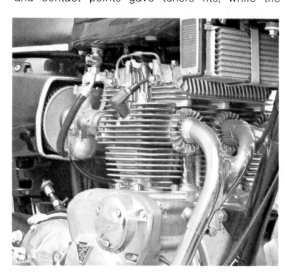

Specification

(1968 model)

engine
Air-cooled, four-stroke, three-cylinder. 67mm (2.63 in.) bore X 70mm (2.75 in.) stroke = 741cc (45 cu.in.). Maximum power 60 bhp at 7250 rpm. Compression ratio 9.5:1. Two valves per cylinder operated via pushrods and rockers by twin camshafts. Three 27mm Amal carburetors

transmission
Four-speed gearbox. Chain drive

frame
Single-down-tube cradle

suspension
Front - Triumph telescopic fork
Rear - Swingarm with Girling coil-over shocks

brakes
Front - Twin-leading-shoe drum (later Lockheed disc)
Rear - Single-leading-shoe drum (later Lockheed disc)

weight
470 lbs. (213kg)

performance
Maximum speed 120 mph
Fuel consumption approximately 40 mpg

The BSA Rocket 3, basically similar to the Trident, used a different frame with the engine inclined slightly forward.

LAVERDA TWIN

Laverda, now one of the prestige names in the superbike market, started by building small economy bikes. It was not until 1968 that they decided to produce a large sports/touring machine. The model featured a 650cc engine with a striking resemblance to the Honda 305 Super Hawk's. But soon after its introduction, praise was heaped on the bike and everyone either forgot about its "look-alike" from Japan or thought it was of no relevance.

Only a handful of these machines were marketed before the Breganze company decided to up the capacity to 744cc and offer the bike in two guises, namely the GT tourer and S sportster.

In endurance racing the 750s were all-conquer-ing in special SFC guise, while a toned-down SF version was made available to the public. The Laverda 750SF is a handsome machine, dominated visually by its tall, heavily finned engine. The power unit is a light-alloy, oversquare 744cc engine canted forward on the crankcase and housing a single overhead camshaft. In 1975 SF form, with twin Dell'Orto 36mm carburetors and an 8.9:1 compression ratio, the engine produces 65 bhp at 7000 rpm. Inside the motor, ball and roller bearings on the crankshaft and camshaft keep all the parts on a friendly basis. All in all, the engine is very smooth for a vertical twin and willing and eager to rev. A triplex primary chain routes the power through a wet, multi-

The overhead-camshaft, twin-cylinder engine of the Laverda 750SF.

plate clutch to a five-speed gearbox and chain final drive. A powerful starter motor is fitted, and this, along with a surprisingly powerful electrical system, makes no fuss of spinning the engine into life.

The engine-and-transmission unit is bolted into a massive spine frame, an interesting feature of which is the absence of front down tubes. However, with the engine used as a stressed member, and a maze of frame tubes under the tank and side panels, there is no doubt as to the strength of the structure. Ceriani suspension is used, utilizing a conventional, but well braced, swingarm at the rear. Earlier models came complete with two massive drum brakes, but in 1975 a Brembo twin-disc setup was used for the front with a twin-leading-shoe 9-in. drum at the rear. Laverda was the first Italian motorcycle manufacturer to dump home-made electrics in favor of Japanese units—the SF certainly is better for it, with complete reliability guaranteed by Nippon Denso instruments and switches. A 4.25-gallon fuel tank is used, while there is a choice of either a twin saddle or Solo type with a sporty hump at the rear. Unfortunately, this leaves room for only the slimmest of passengers.

In all, the 750SF Laverda is a compact, neat package, and very refined for what is still "merely a twin." The biggest surprise of the specification however, is the bike's weight—a colossal 500 lbs. dry. That's not a lot by today's standards, but for a 750 twin it is considerable—its sister 1000cc triple is only about 15 lbs. heavier. The SF does feel fairly small once the rider is seated.

Firing the engine is quite a simple affair, made all the easier with the aid of a handlebar-mounted choke lever. Once warmed up, the idle speed is an unfussed 1000 rpm. Still, the engine is eager to accelerate up to its 8000-rpm red line. Handling at low speeds is quite heavy, due to the steering being set up for higher speeds. Once above 30 mph, the rider is aware of that fact and, as if by magic, the handling gets lighter and inspires great confidence. Roadholding and braking are excellent, while the engine is strong enough to pull the bike's weight up to a speed just under 120 mph and through the timing lights in the quarter mile in a tad under 14 seconds. Fuel consumption is good too, with 50 mpg always possible. An incredible 60 mpg is available when a light throttle is employed. The only criticism of riding is the right-foot gearchange—like that on most other Laverdas, it is notchy and very

The racy lines of the 1976 Laverda 750SF.

Specification

(1975 model)

engine
Air-cooled, four-stroke, twin-cylinder. 80mm (3.15 in.) bore X 74mm (2.91 in.) stroke = 744cc (45 cu.in.). Maximum power 65 bhp at 7000 rpm. Compression ratio 8.9:1. Two valves per cylinder operated via rockers by a single overhead camshaft. Two 36mm Dell'Orto carburetors

transmission
Five-speed gearbox. Chain drive

frame
Four-tube spine using engine as stressed member

suspension
Front - Ceriani telescopic forks
Rear - Swingarm with Ceriani coil-over shocks

brakes
Front - Single Brembo disc (two optional)
Rear - Twin-leading-shoe Brembo drum

weight
500 lbs. (227kg)

performance
Maximum speed 118 mph
Fuel consumption approximately 51 mpg

Jeff Wade in action on his twin-cylinder Laverda during the Formula 750 TT event of 1972.

heavy indeed. Finding neutral requires a bit of forceful tap dancing.

A GTL version of the 750, with a mere 52 bhp, was available as a touring alternative. The fabled SFC on the other hand, had a power output of 75 bhp, triple disc brakes, clip-ons, rear-sets, nose spoiler and a reputation for being not so much a road bike that could win races but a racing bike that could be ridden on roads.

HONDA CB750

The CB750, the 120-mph roadster introduced by Honda in 1969.

Although there have been many machines retrospectively dubbed "superbike," the term is a relatively recent addition to motorcycling jargon. It was coined towards the end of the '60s when the major Japanese factories flooded the market with a whole range of phenomenally quick and powerful machines.

The Honda CB750 was not the first bike to which the term was applied—that honor going to the Triumph and BSA triples—but the model is now regarded as the archetypal, mass-produced superbike. It was a genuine 120-mph roadster with a remarkably sophisticated ride, stunning acceleration, near-perfect braking and reasonable fuel consumption.

The CB750 Honda was first shown to the public at the Tokyo Show in 1968. It featured a 736cc, single-overhead-camshaft, four-cylinder engine which churned out 67 bhp at 8000 rpm, at the time an astonishing figure, and still a fairly respectable amount. The turbine-smooth engine was allied to a slick, five-speed gearbox and included the usual reliable electrics and self-starter. The machine also sported the industry's first mass-produced disc brake. All in all, the bike represented a remarkable standard of technical achievement at a price most enthusiasts could afford.

Backed up by Honda's first-class, worldwide dealer network, it's no surprise the big Honda soon became one of the company's most successful models and has remained so for more than a decade. In the years after the original CB750 was introduced, a number of modifications were made to improve the model even further. The CB750 was not without its faults, however. The bike's handling was indifferent, suffering from the traditional over-sprung/underdamped rear suspension, nylon-bushed swingarm and an overall weight exceeding 500 lbs. Nevertheless, these drawbacks were not nearly enough to deter thousands of would-be owners, so the CB750 always sold like the proverbial hot cakes.

During the decade that has passed since its introduction, a couple of sports versions—the F1 and F2 models—also evolved from the original, and these proved very popular. Gradually, the original K-type became less an outright road burner and more an all-purpose tourer. Even so it was no slouch. A top speed of 120 mph was always available, and any machine capable of covering a quarter-mile in

less than 13 seconds could hardly be described as sluggish.

If the Honda CB750 proved anything, it was that the motorcycling world was crying out for a sophisticated, high-speed tourer that needed an absolute minimum of maintenance and offered sports-car performance for a fraction of the price. That the bike turned a few heads was also a plus.

Perhaps the best description of the CB750 came from an American road tester who summed up the machine as an "iron fist in a velvet glove." Certainly the introduction of the CB750 was a landmark in motorcycling, and perhaps too, it was the first machine that could truly lay claim to the title "superbike."

Specification

(1969 model)

engine
Air-cooled, four-stoke, four-cylinder.
61mm (2.40 in.) bore
X 63mm (2.48 in.) stroke
= 736cc (45 cu.in.). Maximum power
67 bhp at 8000 rpm. Compression
ratio 9.0:1. Two valves per cylinder
operated via rockers by a single
overhead camshaft. Four 28mm
Keihin carburetors

transmission
Five-speed gearbox. Chain drive

frame
Duplex cradle

suspension
Front - Showa telescopic fork
Rear - Swingarm with Showa coil-
over shocks

brakes
Front - Single Honda disc
Rear - Drum

weight
526 lbs. (239kg)

performance
Maximum speed 120 mph
Fuel consumption approximately
42 mpg

this page and opposite Various views of the Honda CB750—the world's first mass-produced superbike—showing (above) its power unit and (left) the tool box under the saddle.

MÜNCH 1200TTS

Normally associated with American taste, the adage "no substitute for cubic inches" must certainly have been close to German Friedl Münch's heart when he set out to build a new motorcycle during the mid-'60s. For maximum performance, Münch decided to use a car engine. After a good look at all the available options he settled for the air-cooled, four-cylinder unit from the NSU Prinz.

Getting his project off the ground was a tricky business, however, and Münch's history is strewn with financial problems, failed partnerships and a great deal of heartache and confusion. Whatever his commercial problems, however, Münch's bikes are well worth a second look.

Probably the best known of all the Münch models is the 1200TTS of the mid-'70s. The power unit was a single-overhead-camshaft 1177cc NSU engine, with two twin-choke Weber carburetors, rated at 88 bhp at 6000 rpm. Later fuel-injected models developed 100 bhp at 7500 rpm. For those who required even more performance, modified 1300cc and even 1400cc versions were available.

In appearance, the 1200TTS was an imposing machine. It carried a large, 5-1/2-gallon fuel tank, giving it a strange hump-backed look, accentuated by its relatively short 55-1/2-inch wheelbase. A nice touch was the addition of a huge all-enclosed final drive chain, complete with its own oil bath. This "chainguard" was interesting for another reason, for it also doubled as the left side of the swingarm.

The 1200TTS used a four-speed gearbox developed from the German Horex Imperator of the late '50s. While effective, the gearchange was somewhat rough—mating a car engine to an obsolete motorcycle gearbox was not without problems. The earliest versions of the Münch were also reputed to handle badly—the combination of a heavy car engine and lightweight frame needed a great deal of sorting to work efficiently.

By the mid-'70s, however, the machine was considerably refined. The handling of the 1200TTS models had improved beyond recognition, but was still hardly in the sports category. A weight of 630 lbs. meant the big machine couldn't be thrown around like a lightweight, and its forte was high-speed cruising. Its roadholding, however, was first class. The rear suspension included highly effective Koni shocks, while the owner had the option of either the British Rickman or Italian Ceriani front forks. Braking was also very effective, the front wheel being equipped with a huge, 12-inch, magnesium drum brake. The last Münch fours had Marzocchi forks and dual front discs, but very few of these were ever made.

By the end of the '70s, recurring financial problems meant that Friedl Münch was forced to sell his company and bring production of his beloved machines to a standstill.

Münch, being a dedicated man, announced details of his new company at the 1978 Cologne Show, and then showed the world his latest creation. It was powered by a 1400cc NSU car engine fitted with a turbocharger and fuel injection, with a claimed power output of 143 bhp. The new bike bore the Horex name, a make that had played an important part in Friedl's life as a young man.

opposite The Münch TTS being put through its paces by a factory tester.

below The four-cylinder Münch outfit of Horst Owesle, winner of the 1971 World Sidecar Championshp.

Specification

(1970 model)

engine
Air-cooled, four-stroke, four-cylinder.
75mm (2.95 in.) bore
X 66.6mm (2.62 in.) stroke
= 1177cc (72 cu.in.). Maximum
power 88 bhp at 6000 rpm.
Compression ratio 8.5:1. Two valves
per cylinder operated via rockers by
a single overhead camshaft. Two
twin-choke 30mm Weber
carburetors

transmission
Four-speed gearbox. Chain drive

frame
Duplex cradle

suspension
Front - Rickman or Ceriani
telescopic fork
Rear - Swingarm with Koni coil-over
shocks

brakes
Front - Twin-leading-shoe Münch
drum (later disc)
Rear - Twin-leading-shoe drum

weight
655 lbs. (297kg)

performance
Maximum speed 125 mph
Fuel consumption approximately
30 mpg

The fuel-injected engine, (top) of the Münch TTS of 1979 (right).

KAWASAKI 750 H2

During the early '70s, so legend has it, there were only two kinds of Kawasaki riders—the quick and the dead. Part of the reason for this somewhat cynical assessment was the arrival of Kawasaki's H1 and H2 three-cylinder, two-stroke road burners.

The H1 introduced in 1969 was a 500cc machine famous for its shattering acceleration, diabolical handling and precious little else. The H1 quickly became a cult machine, particularly in the U.S., and eventually provided the inspiration for the 750cc H2.

If the H1 was a breathtaking performer, the H2 was even more so. At best the H2 was a handful. It had the manners of a bad-tempered stallion and a ride to match. The acceleration was awesome; the handling awful. It was a machine made to be ridden in a straight line, and even then only by the brave and sensible. Riders grabbing an injudicious handful of throttle were rewarded with a period of truly knuckle-whitening terror as the H2 catapulted its front wheel into the air. This same maneuver attempted in anything other than a straight line was virtually guaranteed to launch machine and rider headlong into the nearest ditch, hence the "quick and dead" legend. With 100 mph arriving in less than 10 seconds, "clutch popping" was an experience few newcomers to the H2 would try more than once.

The main reason for the H2's eye-widening performance was its power-to-weight ratio. The machine weighed only 450 lbs., but its three-cylinder, air-cooled, 748cc, two-stroke engine punched out 74 bhp at 6800 rpm—sufficient to blast the machine through a quarter-mile in 12.5 seconds and give it a top speed around 125 mph. The truth of the matter, however, was the H2 had too much engine for its own good. The lightweight frame simply was not up to coping with the stresses transmitted through it.

Weight distribution, with a distinct rearward bias, gave excellent traction and a light front end—a combination that helped produce those spectacular wheelies. The machine's temperament was not helped by the fact that the H2's engine was decidedly peaky. The violent power meant that keeping the front wheel on the ground was a major problem. It was a vicious circle and quite naturally the H2 came to be regarded as a machine not to be trifled with.

The performance softened a bit over the years and the bike became more tractable, but by the mid-'70s the H2 was no more. Poor fuel consumption—at its best, the H2 could only cover 30 miles on a gallon—and threatening emission regulations killed it off. Ironically, by this time, attempts had been made to tame the beast. The frame had been lengthened, the fork rake increased, the engine repositioned and the rear-suspension units improved. Even so the H2 was still a spectacular machine to ride and still simply too wild to tame properly.

Today the Kawasaki H2 has become one of motorcycling's classic Japanese machines. It was one of a range of remarkable models on which Kawasaki built its early reputation. Time has mellowed the memory regarding the H2's many faults, but for those who rode the H2, the image of the howling, smoking two-stroke will remain forever imprinted on their minds—or bodies.

Mick Grant riding his three-cylinder 750 during the trans-Atlantic races at Brands Hatch in 1978.

The 750 H2 that must have taken many a new rider's breath away.

Specification

(1970 model)

engine
Air-cooled, two-stroke, three-cylinder. 71mm (2.79 in.) bore X 63mm (2.48 in.) stroke = 748cc (46 cu.in.). Maximum power 74 bhp at 6800 rpm. Compression ratio 7.0:1. Three 32mm Mikuni carburetors

transmission
Five-speed gearbox.

Chain drive
frame
Duplex cradle
suspension
Front - Kayaba telescopic fork
Rear - Swingarm with Kayaba coil-over shocks
brakes
Front - Single Kawasaki disc (twin optional)

Rear - Drum
weight
430 lbs. (195kg)
performance
Maximum speed 125 mph
Fuel consumption approximately 30 mpg

SUZUKI GT750

It was during the early '70s that the superbike war between the major Japanese factories broke out. Honda had already introduced the four-cylinder CB750 in 1969 and was not long before Suzuki weighed in with their new superbike contender. Suzuki, however, took a completely different route with their machine, the GT750.

For a start, their bike was a two-stroke, at 750cc the largest two-stroke ever mass produced. In addition, the engine had three cylinders and was water-cooled. Although originally marketed as a direct rival to the Honda CB750, it soon became obvious that the Suzuki lacked the outright performance of the Honda. Eventually the GT750 found its own niche as a high-speed tourer.

The internals of the unit were quite straightforward; piston porting, a roller-bearing crankshaft, oversquare bore and stroke, and triple 32mm slide-needle carburetors. Water-cooling, apart from keeping the engine at an even temperature, gave the all-alloy unit a very unconventional appearance indeed as it didn't demand conventional finning.

Although early models were sluggish performers, the later M-series LeMans were relatively quick. The addition of 40mm constant-vacuum carburetors and more radical port timing gave the engine enough performance to make the power claimed for the F750 Suzukis more believable. In racing tune, the engine was rated near 115 bhp, and the Formula 750s of Suzuki were forces to be reckoned with in Europe and the United States.

With a 6.9:1 compression ratio, the M-series engine produced a respectable 67 bhp at 6500 rpm and a thumping 62 lbs.ft. of torque at 5500 rpm. Even more impressive was the power delivery. The engine had a remarkably flat power band, and response was along the lines normally associated with four strokes. This was apparent on the road; the GT750 was a very smooth bike with no peakiness to catch an unwary rider offguard.

An electric starter was fitted to the GT, and once running the engine idled quite smoothly at just over 1000 rpm. Throttle response was instantaneous and it was quite easy to overstep the redline. Acceleration from a standing start was quite impressive, but accompanied by quite a lot of blue smoke from the four exhaust pipes. The quarter mile took just 13.3 seconds, with a terminal speed just over 100 mph. Although not quite in the same league as the later four-stroke GS750, this was still respectable for a three-quarter-liter bike built primarily as a tourer.

Fuel consumption was excellent, with an average around 40 mpg possible. Driven gently, the bike could produce a remarkable 55—60 mpg. A touring range around 200 miles could be expected with the 3.75-gallon fuel tank. Although the engine was very smokey, particularly when accelerating, oil consumption was quite reasonable, about 300 miles per pint. An oil-tank capacity of 3.2 pints gave the bike a range of 900 miles or better.

The most disappointing feature of the Suzuki was its handling. On smooth roads it was adequate until the speed increased. High speeds, however, revealed a certain limpness in the chassis. Rough surfaces accentuated the problem, and progress could become a very hair-raising affair. Riders who held on were rewarded with another surprise—poor cornering clearance. Any one of a number of bits could be stuffed into the pavement, but the side and center stands were the major culprits.

Twin discs at the front gave the machine ferocious braking, but they were prone to hesitation in wet weather. Luckily the rear drum gave adequate braking for the 540-lb. machine while the front discs were drying out.

Like many two-strokes, the GT750 fell victim to the encroaching emission regulations of the mid-'70s, but there were a number of riders who mourned the passing of Suzuki's "water-buffalo."

opposite Being water-cooled, the GT750 has a prominent radiator.

right The neat layout of the Suzuki GT750 instrument panel.

Specification

(1975 model)

engine
Water-cooled, two-stroke, three-cylinder. 70mm (2.75 in.) bore X 64mm (2.52 in.) stroke = 738cc (45 cu.in.). Maximum power 67 bhp at 6500 rpm. Compression ratio 6.9:1. Three 40mm Mikuni CV carburetors

transmission
Five-speed gearbox. Chain drive

frame
Duplex cradle

suspension
Front - Shoei telescopic fork
Rear - Swingarm with Kayaba coil-over shocks

brakes
Front - Twin Suzuki discs
Rear - Drum

weight
540 lbs. (245kg)

performance
Maximum speed 120 mph
Fuel consumption approximately 44 mpg

top Three Mikuni CV carburetors feed the 750cc GT Suzuki engine.

right Although heavy, the GT750 is very quick and quite maneuverable.

BENELLI 750 SEI

For years, four-cylinder motorcycles were considered the ultimate in sophisticated motorcycling, but by 1974, fours were becoming *de rigeuer* for any serious manufacturer. At this time, Benelli announced what was considered by some the next logical step in sophistication—a six. Although no longer the only six-cylinder roadster, the Benelli 750 Sei was, by far, the first.

To a large degree the machine reflected the changes brought by Benelli's new owner, Alejandro de Tomaso. Not only was the Sei worlds away from the marque's famous racers and twin-cylinder roadsters, was also a bit extravagant compared to the Japanese superbikes.

Heart of the big Benelli is the straight-six, seven-main-bearing engine. Its bore and stroke are 56mm X 50.6mm—figures Honda enthusiasts may recognize as the dimensions of the four-cylinder Honda 500 engine, for it was from that unit that the Sei was developed. In fact, in profile, the Italian engine looks nearly identical to its Japanese counterpart.

Like the Honda, the Benelli has a single overhead camshaft, chain-driven from the center of the crank. The camshaft actuates rockers for the two valves per cylinder. Crankshaft whip is reduced by having the power take-off from the center of the crank, and

the drive goes via a multi-plate clutch to a five-speed gearbox with chain final drive. The perfect primary and secondary balance of a straight-six makes for a very smooth unit, and the Benelli is no exception. It accelerates from idle to maximum power with no fuss or vibration. Maximum power is 71 bhp at 8900 rpm, which suggests that the 748cc engine is in a moderate state of tune.

To give adequate cornering clearance with the engine's width, designer Lino Tonti set the engine high in the duplex frame. Still, the high center of gravity has little adverse effect on the Sei's handling.

Styling is probably the Sei's weakest point, for it is rather plain with high handlebars flanking an oblong instrument panel. The size of the large, five-gallon, tank has been cunningly disguised by having the frontal portion painted black to break up the line. Although the exhaust system fanning out into six separate tail pipes looks impressive, it is a bit dated. Perhaps these days when one piece tank/seat/fairing units and alloy wheels are common, the Sei does show its age a little.

Tipping the scales at a dry weight of just 485 lbs., the big Benelli belies its bulky looks. On the open road, all thoughts of size and weight are forgotten, for the Benelli handles really well and corners at astonishing speed. In no way does the bike lose any of its impeccable Italian-style road manners, a portion of which can be attributed to the Marzocchi suspension. Braking is on a par with the handling, with twin Brembo cast-iron discs at the front and a powerful drum at the rear.

The Sei's performance is excellent, with a top speed of just over 120 mph and standing-start quarter-mile acceleration of 12.9 seconds. Not surprisingly, fuel consumption depends a great deal on how the bike is ridden. If the throttle is feathered, over 50 mpg can be obtained, but this figure will drop to under 30 mpg if the engine is kept spinning hard. Unfortunately for the riders' finances, the engine note encourages the use of the lowest possible gear and the highest possible engine speed. In performance, handling, style and price, the Benelli may not be the Ferrari of motorcycles; but the sound of its engine certainly conjures up visions of those fabulous cars. In that respect at least, it has no competition.

right The Sei handles well and corners quickly and efficiently.

opposite Styling is probably its weakest point.

above The characteristic fan of the Sei's exhaust system is an impressive reminder of its six-cylinder engine, the first to be introduced in the motorcycle market.

right The heart of the machine is this single-overhead-camshaft, 747cc engine.

The six cylinders are fed by three Dell'Orto carburetors.

Specification

(1975 model)

engine
Air-cooled, four-stroke, six-cylinder. 56mm (2.20 in.) bore X 50.6mm (1.99 in.) stroke = 748cc (46 cu.in.). Maximum power 71 bhp at 8900 rpm. Compression ratio 9.0:1. Two valves per cylinder operated via rockers by a single overhead camshaft. Three 24mm Dell'Orto carburetors

transmission
Five-speed gearbox. Chain drive

frame
Duplex cradle

suspension
Front - Marzocchi telescopic fork
Rear - Swingarm with Marzocchi coil-over shocks

brakes
Front - Twin Brembo discs
Rear - Brembo drum

weight
485 lbs. (219kg)

performance
Maximum speed 121 mph
Fuel consumption approximately 35 mpg

NORTON COMMANDO

The vertical-twin is an integral part of British motorcycling history, and in recent years the two mainstays of the British industry, the Triumph Bonneville and Norton Commando, relied on this layout.

Although basically similar to the Triumph, the Norton engine had a reputation as a "torquer." The long stroke made the Norton decidedly "undersquare," and it became one of the major contributors to the long-stroke/high-torque myth.

The engine became rather breathless above 6000 rpm, which in a way was fortunate. The huge, full-circle flywheel was mounted between the cylinders, supported only by two outboard main bearings. Riders who continuously over-revved the engine usually wound up limping home with expensive noises emanating from the engine's innards. The engine used the British standard pushrod-and-rocker valve system, along with a mild 8.5:1 compression ratio. The Commando was not short of power, however, and developed 58 bhp at 5900 rpm from its 828cc, enough to give it very respectable performance.

The engine also played an unusual role in the design of the frame. Mounted in the disastrous Norton Atlas in the '60s, the 745cc engine acquired such a well-deserved reputation for vibration that it became obvious that something had to be done. In a brilliant engineering *non sequitur*, Norton redesigned the frame.

The "Isolastic" frame was a complete departure from the legendary "Featherbed" unit used on the works Norton racers. The Commando frame was tall and narrow, featuring rubber mountings for the engine, transmission and swingarm. The mounting system allowed the engine/transmission to hop like a spastic frog at idle, but above 2000 rpm the bike was surprisingly smooth. Despite the amount of rubber in the drivetrain, the big Norton was very much at home on twisty roads, with its well-designed steering no doubt helping to make it handle neutrally and safely.

The engine was coupled to a four-speed gearbox which, even with the ample power available, still had one ratio too few. But the gearchanges and clutch action were remarkably light, and made for quick and fuss-free cog swapping.

Despite a displacement increase from 745cc to 828cc, the last Mk II Commandos were somewhat tamer than their predecessors. Top speed of the Mk II was, however, a creditable 110 mph with a standing-start quarter-mile time of just over 14 seconds. Average fuel consumption was 45 mpg, and consumption did not drop much below that figure even when the bike was ridden hard.

In its waning years the Norton company was pandering to the dictates of the American market. This was emphasized by the machine's electric-start system. For years, Norton enthusiasts developed strong right legs for starting their machines. But Americans were spoiled by 20th-Century electrics from Japan, so demanded a pushbutton starter. A system was fitted—the only problem was that it was hardly enough to spin two 414cc cylinders.

Although in its Mk II guise the Commando was not as quick as its predecessors, it was still a well-loved and capable machine. NVT, however, decided to concentrate on the more modern Triumph Trident, so the Commando was quietly dropped. Not long after, the Trident went out of production. The Norton name was left for the Wankel-engined bike, and later, the Cosworth/Norton—both of which eventually withered before seeing the light of day.

right Dave Croxford in action on his 750 Norton during the 1973 season.

opposite 1967 saw the production of the new Norton twin, the Commando. This is the last of this famous line, the 850 MK II.

right A single rear disk brake and Girling coil-over shocks were used on the 850 Commando.

far right Instrumentation on the Commando.

below right The Commando engine was mounted in an innovative frame, using the famous Norton Isolastic system.

An early 750cc
Commando.

Specification

(1975 model)

engine
Air-cooled, four-stroke, twin-cylinder.
77mm (3.03 in.) bore
X 89mm (3.50 in.) stroke
= 828cc (50 cu.in.). Maximum power
58 bhp at 5900 rpm. Compression
ratio 8.5:1. Two valves per cylinder
operated via pushrods and rockers
by a single, rear-mounted camshaft.
Two 32mm Amal carburetors
transmission
Four-speed gearbox. Chain drive
frame
Duplex cradle
suspension
Front - Norton telescopic fork

Rear - Swingarm with Girling
coil-over shocks
brakes
Front - Single Lockheed disc
Rear - Single Lockheed disc
weight
430 lbs. (195kg)
performance
Maximum speed 110 mph
Fuel consumption approximately
45 mpg

SUZUKI RE5

The instrument cluster (above) used on the early 1974 Suzuki RE5 (right).

During the early '70s, the Wankel engine was being touted as the engine of the future. Several car manufacturers, including GM, had extensive development programs underway and both Mazda and NSU had models already available. Suzuki and Yamaha put the rotary engine on two wheels. Although Yamaha stopped their program in the prototype stage, Suzuki went into production.

After more than a year of hints and rumors, the RE5 was finally announced in 1974. The public was taken aback, not only by its revolutionary engine but also with its "zoomy," futuristic styling. Heart of the bike was a transverse-mounted, single-rotor Wankel engine. Running a 9.4:1 compression ratio and a swept volume of 497cc, the engine produced a respectable 62 bhp at 6500 rpm and a very healthy 54.9 lbs.ft. of torque at 3500 rpm. A wet, multiplate clutch was fitted, along with a five-speed gearbox and chain drive.

Although the basic idea of a Wankel is very simple, the installation involves a good deal of complexity, and the Suzuki reflected it. Much of it was due to the heat generated by the engine; the bike featured water cooling, oil cooling and, ridiculous as it sounds, muffler cooling. In addition to the standard four-stroke lubrication system, a two-stroke-type oil-injection system, requiring a separate oil tank, was used for the critical apex seals. The large radiator and bulky engine gave the RE5 a solid and heavy look. The look was confirmed by a dry weight of 565 lbs.—heavy by normal standards and gross for a "500."

The initial impression when one first started the RE5 was that it was quite noisy, and certainly not as smooth as expected. Once above its 1500-rpm idle, however, the motor didn't feel quite so lumpy. It was quite easy to zap the engine up to its 7000-rpm red line. Despite a staged, two-barrel carburetor, throttle response was a little sluggish. It wasn't until the second throat opened that any hint of power was realized. Acceleration off the line was about par for a 500, with a quarter mile coming up in just under 14 seconds. Top speed was 110 mph, but with the machine's frontal area and weight, a bit of patience and a lot of pavement was needed to reach it.

The old rotary bugaboo, fuel consumption, was the RE5's fatal flaw. It was hard to better 35 mpg. Overzealous use of the right hand could drop that figure well into the 20s, poor for any motorcycle and abysmal for a 500. The bike's fuel tank, with a mere

3.6-gallon capacity, crippled the bike as a high-speed tourer.

As for handling, the bike was a preview of Suzuki's future models. It was one of the first good-handling Japanese motorcycles. It could still be upset by the combination of high speed and lumpy corners, but as a tourer the bike handled well. The weight and high center of gravity tended to slow transitional response, but once set on a line, the bike cornered quite well. Braking was taken care of by twin discs at the front and a drum at the rear. Although they were exceptional in the dry, there was a marked hesitation when the front discs were wet.

The early RE5s featured odd cylindrical instrument nacelles and taillights, but units from the GT750 were later used in the hope that a slightly more conventional-looking bike would attract more buyers. Unfortunately, it was high fuel consumption and poor range, not styling, that doomed the bike's acceptance. Its future dimmed with the first hints of the gas shortage. Even in restyled, RE5A form, the bike was not a success and in 1977 it was quietly dropped, with little fuss and virtually no mourners.

above The RE5 model produced in 1977 incorporated several modifications.

right A cut-away drawing of the RE5's rotary engine.

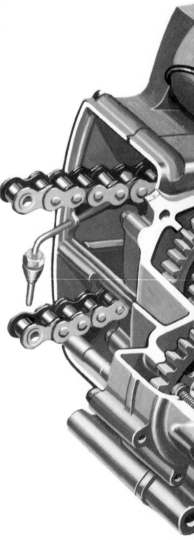

Specification

(1976 model)

engine
Water-cooled, single-rotor, Wankel. Swept volume 497cc (30 cu.in.). Maximum power 62 bhp at 6500 rpm. Compression ratio 9.4:1. Single, staged 18/32mm two-barrel Mikuni HHD carburetor

transmission
Five-speed gearbox. Chain drive

frame
Duplex cradle

suspension
Front - Shoei telescopic fork
Rear - Swingarm with Kayaba coil-over shocks

brakes
Front - Twin Suzuki discs
Rear - Drum

weight
565 lbs. (257kg)

performance
Maximum speed 110 mph
Fuel consumption approximately 32 mpg

VAN VEEN OCR1000

Henk van Veen first came to the notice of the motorcycling press when he built the tiny Kreidler-engined racer on which fellow Dutchman Henk van Kessel won the 50cc world title in 1972. He followed this up by shoehorning a Wankel Mazda car engine into a Moto Guzzi frame and proclaiming that he wanted to put such a bike into production. If that doesn't sound like a logical proposition it is probably because van Veen doesn't always do things logically. He does like to do things properly, however; indeed, Henk van Veen is a man driven by a dream to create the perfect motorcycle.

The Mazda-engined Van Veen made its appearance around 1972, and development continued for a couple of years. Eventually, the Mazda engine was dropped and a new limited-production model, the OCR1000, made its debut at the '74 Cologne Show.

The OCR1000 was a fascinating machine. It used a double-rotor Wankel engine developed by van Veen and the Citroen-owned company, Comotor. Each rotor swept a volume of 498cc, giving the engine a total displacement of 996cc. Perhaps the most impressive statistic, however, was the Van Veen's power output—100 bhp at 6500 rpm. A top speed of 150 mph was claimed, but it was not the ourtright performance of which van Veen was most proud. His ambition was to create a quality machine—the ultimate superbike—and the OCR1000 was certainly close. The machines were virtually handmade, and as a result, they were both remarkably well finished and frightfully expensive.

The frame of the big OCR was designed by Jaap Voskamp, and used front forks and rear suspension units from Koni. The gearbox and drive shaft were developed in conjunction with Porsche. To stop the machine, which weighed a colossal 700 lbs. plus, twin Brembo discs were used at the front and a single disc at the rear.

Weight wasn't the only colossal specification; van Veen's dream to create the ultimate superbike meant that the machine was expensive. By 1977, an OCR1000 cost about £5500 in Britain, a price that had escalated to £7000 only a year later. Henk van

The 1979 OCR1000 Van Veen (right). Unlike previous models, a fairing was fitted (opposite).

Veen refused to compromise, however, and the OCR1000 became a much coveted status symbol.

Very few OCR1000 models ever found their way into the hands of press road testers, but those that did obviously left a vivid impression. The incredible power output of the rotary engine meant that opening the throttle wide was an impressive undertaking, 0 to 125 mph in just 16 seconds. The claimed top speed of 150 mph usually proved to be an exaggeration, but more than one test rider saw 135 mph. The most impressive sensation, however, was the smooth and certain way the OCR1000 would pull from walking speed in almost any gear.

In the end, the economics of producing such a machine proved too much for Henk van Veen's little factory and, at the beginning of 1979, the company announced that no more of the glorious OCRs would be built. By this stage, van Veen was quoting a British price of £10,000 (about $22,000, give or take cab fare) for his machine—at that rate there were few takers. This was one dream machine too few could afford.

A Van Veen test rider tries out an early OCR1000.

Two views of the Rotary engine. The inside (left) and the outside (above).

Specification

(1975 model)

engine
Water-cooled, twin-rotor, Wankel.
Swept volume 996cc (61 cu.in.).
Maximum power 100 bhp at 6500
rpm. Single staged two-barrel Solex
carburetor

transmission
Four-speed gearbox. Shaft drive

frame
Duplex cradle

suspension
Front - Koni telescopic fork
Rear - Swingarm with Koni coil-over
shocks

brakes
Front - Twin Brembo discs
Rear - Single Brembo disc

weight
650 lbs. (295kg)

performance
Maximum speed 140 mph
Fuel consumption approximately
30 mpg

MOTO GUZZI LE MANS

In the late '60s, Moto Guzzi introduced the V7 series, using a 90° V-twin engine mounted longitudinally in the frame. The layout made it quite easy to build the bikes with shaft drive. The machines became very popular, especially with the Italian army and police forces.

The most attractive variation on the V7 theme was the S3 Sports. Fitted with low-set bars, a sports saddle and rear-set pegs, the 750cc machine was soon heralded as one of the best-looking bikes available. It was also capable of a top speed above 120 mph.

Built on the same lines as its predecessor, the Le Mans was launched in 1975. The heart of the bike is an 844cc engine producing a very healthy 81 bhp at 7600 rpm. That figure is impressive enough, but doesn't really convey exactly what the engine is like. As the crank is longitudinally mounted, a blip of the throttle at standstill will tip the bike slightly to the right—much like a BMW. But the Guzzi motor uses twin 36mm carburetors and a hefty 10.2:1 compression ratio, giving it a feel and sound a lot more brutal than that of the German machine.

Power is routed through a dry twin-plate clutch to a five-speed gearbox and shaft drive. Gear change is quite easy with a very light action, although extra care has to be taken when changing down to lower gears. The engine and transmission sit in a large duplex frame, with the sump hanging down between the bottom tubes. This helps give the bike a low center of gravity.

In fact the whole bike is exceptionally low, with a seat height of just over 30 inches. The Le Mans has what is almost a cafe-racer riding position, with the rider leaning forward to the bars. Passengers have little choice but to sit upright and square to the airstream.

Suspension is conventional, but the braking is taken care of by the patented Moto-Guzzi integral system. The foot pedal actuates front and rear brakes. A proportioning valve distributes 75 per cent of braking effort to the front disc and 25 per cent to the rear unit. The bar-mounted lever actuates the other front disc. The linked system is so efficient that once the rider gets used to using the right foot for most situations—something not

Tony Osbourne's production racing Moto Guzzi 850 in action at Thruxton in 1976.

recommended on an ordinary bike—the handlebar-mounted brake lever becomes almost redundant. To quote the factory literature "the other disc should be used in emergencies and 'sports riding.'" However they are used, there is never difficulty in stopping the 431-lb. machine in the wet or dry.

The machine is geared fairly high, giving the bike an impressive top speed of 125 mph, but hampering acceleration somewhat. Quarter-mile time is just under 14 seconds. As for fuel consumption, the high gearing enhances it, with a figure always hovering around the 35—40-mpg mark and occasionally rising above it.

The original Le Mans was replaced by the Le Mans II, sporting a 1000cc engine, larger nose fairing, revised instruments and some extra bodywork

around the cylinders. The revised looks, however, cannot disguise the brutal nature of a very capable and thoroughbred machine.

The big Guzzi sports three cross-drilled brake discs, operated by the company's well-known integral system.

above The original Le Mans used a massive, transverse-mounted 844cc V-twin.

opposite The bike's saddle is quite low at 30.5 inches from the ground. When on the machine, the rider leans forward over the tank and positions himself comfortably behind the small fairing.

Specification

(1978 model)

engine
Air-cooled, four-stroke, V-twin.
83mm (3.26 in.) bore
X 78mm (3.07 in.) stroke
= 844cc (52 cu.in.). Maximum power
81 bhp at 7600 rpm. Compression
ratio 10.2:1. Two valves per cylinder
operated via pushrods and rockers
by a single central camshaft. Two
36mm Dell'Orto carburetors

transmission
Five-speed gearbox. Shaft drive

frame
Duplex cradle

suspension
Front - Moto Guzzi telescopic fork
Rear - Swingarm with Moto Guzzi
coil-over shocks

brakes
Front - Twin Brembo discs
Rear - Single Brembo disc with
integral linked system

weight
485 lbs. (220kg)

performance
Maximum speed 125 mph
Fuel consumption approximately
38 mpg

DUCATI 900SS

Of all the superbikes in current production, the Ducati 900SS is probably the lightest and most sparsely equipped. But enthusiasts of the marque will assert those features are its virtues; the 900SS is a no-frills thoroughbred.

The heart of the bike is a 90° V-twin engine, mounted with the front cylinder a few degrees above horizontal. This layout has several advantages. It gives the machine a low center of gravity, moves engine weight forward for better weight distribution, and gives the rear cylinder an unobstructed air stream. The narrow engine also gives a small frontal area and good cornering clearance. At high speeds especially, a narrow engine is equivalent to a considerable horsepower advantage over a transverse multi. The major disadvantage to the 90° layout is its odd look, and for that reason few manufacturers have used it.

The name Fabio Taglioni is well known to Ducatiphiles, and the 900SS engine bears his trademark—desmodromic valves. Instead of using coil springs or torsion bars for closing the valves, the

The lightweight 900 Super Sport uses the famous Ducati desmodromic system.

"desmo" system features direct valve closure by a second cam lobe and rocker. The system allows the engine to rev higher without heavy valve springs to control valve float. While current "desmos" feature lightweight, hairpin springs to ensure that the valves seat properly during starting, the engines do quite well without them, thank you.

As can be imagined, such a system is expensive, and it also has other disadvantages. The main one is that frequent attention has to be paid to valve adjustment; it is wise to check valve clearances every 500 miles. Although many of the advantages of the system have been rendered unnecessary by modern valve springs, the magic of desmodromics remains. Ducatis have desmodromic valves because that's what Ducati makes, and people expect them.

In European trim, the 864cc engine has a 9.5:1 compression ratio and breathes through two enormous 40mm slide-needle Dell'Orto carburetors. The exhaust system on the bike is designed to enhance performance, rather than simply suppress noise,

The rear suspension consists of a swingarm with Marzocchi shocks and adjustable concentric springs. Alloy rims were later replaced with magnesium wheels.

and gives out a very throaty roar. This, together with rudimentary flame guards over the carburetor intakes, makes the bike very noisy. Although the exhaust and 40mm carburetors are optional, the US model is equipped with 32mm Dell'Ortos, air filters, and a more restrictive, but quieter, exhaust.

The company does not disclose power outputs, but the Ducati 900SS can probably manage close to 70 bhp, produced near its 7900-rpm redline, and a maximum of 55 lbs.ft. of torque. As expected, the US version is below these figures, but the machine has a fatter midrange, giving a remarkably tractable engine.

The 900SS weighs just 414 lbs., a fact that

Specification

(1979 model)

engine
Air-cooled, four-stroke, V-twin.
86mm (3.38 in.) bore X 74.4mm
(2.92 in.) stroke = 864cc (52.75
cu.in.). Maximum power 70 bhp at
7000 rpm. Compression ratio 9.5:1.
Two valves per cylinder operated
via desmodromic gear by a single
overhead camshaft. Two 40mm
Dell'Orto carburetors

transmission
Five-speed gearbox. Chain drive

frame
Twin-down-tube using engine as
stressed member

suspension
Front - Marzocchi telescopic fork
Rear - Swingarm with Marzocchi
coil-over shocks

brakes
Front - Twin Brembo discs
Rear - Single Brembo disc

weight
414 lbs. (188kg)

performance
Maximum speed 132mph
Fuel consumption approximately
46 mpg

reflects Ducati's attitude toward performance—the key is power-to-weight, not just horsepower. A variety of sprockets is available, the most long-legged of which gives the bike a theoretical top speed of 152 mph. In practice, however, the most one can expect from the bike is just over 130 mph. Acceleration again depends on gearing, but a standing-start quarter-mile time of a little over 12 seconds is possible.

In addition to spectacular performance, the Ducati is capable of returning more than 60 mpg if a light hand is used on the throttle. An average of 40 mpg can still be expected even if full use is made of the performance.

The engine is used as a stressed member, with two down tubes running from the steering head to the crankcase. The remainder of the frame is large-diameter tubing, and is as rigid as the engine. This

John Chappell on board the Ducati 900SS Desmo production racer in 1976.

keeps the Compagnolo magnesium wheels in line and contributes to the bike's superb handling; in fact, it is probably the best handling production roadster made. With the low weight and the sticky Pirelli tires, cornering is better than just about anything else on the road.

Switches and instrumentation are fair, but not up to recent standards of Italian bikes; something a Ducati owner simply has to put up with. A strong right leg is also needed. Unlike the other desmo models in the Ducati range, the 900SS has no electric starter—a starter motor would add weight.

BMW R100RS

How do you put a price on prestige and quality? If someone built a motorcycle with a pushrod, twin-cylinder engine with a basic design decades old, then priced it a several thousand dollars higher than its rivals, would it sell? All logic says it shouldn't. But that's exactly what BMW does, and the company sells every bike they can build.

BMWs have proven their quality and dependability over the years. Although the company doesn't produce a great many bikes, their exclusivity, quality and high price have given BMW the kind of image usually associated with Rolls-Royce, caviar and European snobbery.

Top of BMW's sport range is the R100RS model, the most remarkable feature of which is its integrated fairing. Developed in the Pininfarina wind tun-

right & opposite The BMW R100RS, well-known for its high-quality finish and reliability.

nel, the fairing is designed for rider protection and to reduce aerodynamic lift, rather than to improve outright top speed. The R100RS was a logical progression for BMW, because its products are best known for their high-speed, long-distance cruising ability. The RS is simply an attempt to create the ultimate sports tourer, whereas the R100RT, with its larger fairing and saddlebags, is the more traditional touring bike.

The R100RS is powered by a horizontally opposed, twin-cylinder 980cc engine. Fitted with two 40mm constant-vacuum Bing carburetors and low-restriction exhaust, the engine develops 70 bhp at 7250 rpm—5 bhp more than the S. This gives the bike a top speed around 125 mph.

Riding the R100RS is an interesting experience. There is a slight boom from the fairing, but the engine is uncannily quiet and smooth. Wind noise is minimal, and as a result is a poor speed indicator— it is wise to keep an eye on the speedometer. In addition, the handling and braking of the big BMW are superb and predictable; even the trickiest of bends can be taken with sure-footed confidence. Some riders worry about grounding the cylinder heads—actually the rocker covers—but the fear is unfounded. The covers have been known to kiss the pavement under racing conditions, but it would take some spectacular gymnastics to do it on the street without laying it down.

When the weather turns nasty, the R100RS comes into its own. The fairing and the excellent Continental tires ensure that rain will have little effect on the machine's high-speed capability or the rider's comfort. The fairing is so effective that wind and rain are diverted around the rider, enabling him to arrive clean and dry.

Apart from its impressive ride, the BMW's other major asset is its excellent range. With a 5-gallon tank and fuel consumption of 50 mpg, the BMW offers hours of uninterrupted travel, a feature so important to the hardened tourer.

A reputation for quality is not something earned overnight; it takes years of producing dependable, no-compromise machines. BMWs are more expensive than most motorcycles, but most owners would argue it just isn't possible to put a price on real class.

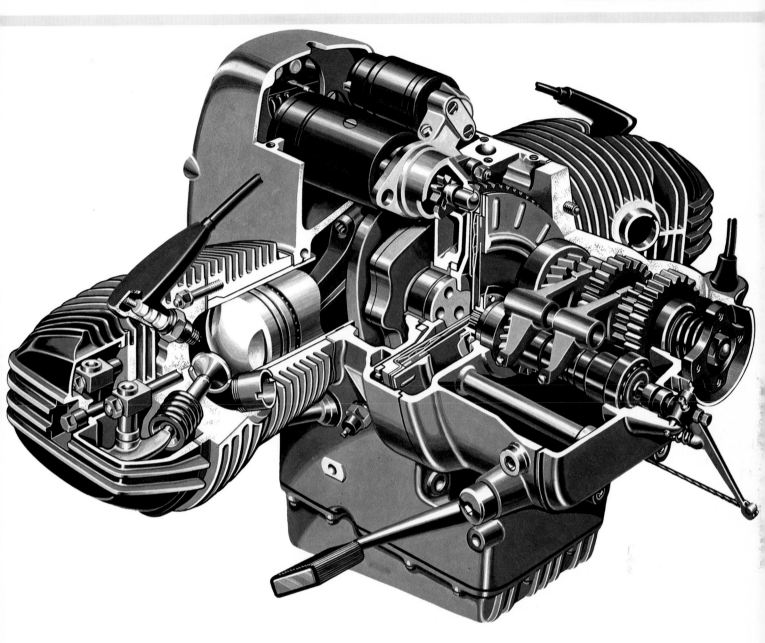

Specification

(1976 model)

engine
Air-cooled, four-stroke, flat-twin. 94mm (3.70 in.) bore X 70.6mm (2.77 in.) stroke = 980cc (60 cu.in.). Maximum power 70 bhp at 7250 rpm. Compression ratio 9.5:1. Two valves per cylinder operated via pushrods and rockers by a single central camshaft. Two 40mm Bing constant-vacuum carburetors

transmission
Five-speed gearbox.
Shaft drive

frame
Duplex cradle
suspension
Front - BMW telescopic fork
Rear - Swingarm with Boge coil-over shocks
brakes
Front - Twin ATE discs
Rear - Drum (later Brembo disc)
weight
500 lbs. (227kg)
performance
Maximum speed 125 mph
Fuel consumption approximately 50 mpg

above A cut-away drawing of the BMW 1000cc engine used in the RS and RT range.

opposite The BMW R100RT, basically the same as the RS except for fairing and saddlebags.

LAVERDA JOTA 1000

There must be something about the air in Italy that inspires Italian engineers to build cars and motorcycles that are so downright exciting. Even the names Ferrari, Maserati, MV Agusta and Laverda have an aura of glamour and excitement.

Since the end of World War II, the Laverda company of Breganze has been making a name for itself by building machines which embodied the high-spirited principles so beloved of the Italians. Indeed, Laverda's current offering in the superbike stakes—the Jota—is the absolute epitome of a superbike.

Ironically, Laverda needed a little British inspiration to produce the Jota. During the mid-'70s, Roger Slater, Laverda's British importer, was campaigning the Italian company's 1000cc 3CE models in production races with great success. But a host of fast, multi-cylinder Japanese superbikes made Slater's natural desire for more performance a pressing need. Laverda complied, and so was born the Jota.

The Jota uses the 3CE's three-cylinder, double-overhead-camshaft engine, but with wilder racing cams, three 32mm Dell'Orto carburetors, a close-ratio gearbox and a modified exhaust system.

The result is an already quick machine became even faster. The Jota is capable of almost 140 mph, while a standing-start quarter mile will take just under 13 seconds. All-out speed, however, is not really what the Jota is about. It is a rider's bike, the kind of machine that comes into its own on fast and twisty roads. The handlebars are set low and narrow and the seat well back, allowing the rider to wrap around the sleek 4-gallon fuel tank.

The engine is not as smooth as that of a Japanese multi, but that is part of the Jota's attraction. To avoid the rocking couple associated with a 120° triple, Laverda places the outer crank throws at 180° to the center one. The "two up, one down, one up, two down" power strokes of the Jota give it a distinct, but peculiar, idle. The engine smooths out just off idle, however, and acceleration is spectacular.

The 1979 Jota included a fairing.

The engine is massively powerful—90 bhp at 7600 rpm.

On the road the Jota has all the manners of a thoroughbred, but it is also tough, brutal and uncompromising. The clutch lever is numbingly stiff, while the five-speed gearbox needs a positive change. The brakes—twin 11-inch Brembo discs at the front, a single disc at the rear—are fierce and positive. The net result is that the Jota is a taut and frill-free machine, definitely not the kind of bike for a Sunday afternoon ride. The engine begs to be revved and the handling makes it difficult to resist throwing the Jota into every corner.

In spite of its road-racer personality, the Laverda sports a surprising number of refinements. It has an electric starter, a generous tool kit, electronic ignition, an easy-to-use main stand and more-than-adequate air horns. In addition, chain wear is remarkably low for such a potent device, a fact that may be due to the correct geometrical relationship between the final-drive sprocket centers and the needle-bearing pivot of the swingarm.

For sheer exhilaration, there can be little to equal the Laverda Jota. It is not cheap, but neither is it prohibitively expensive. In any case, most Jota owners would say the sheer joy of riding such a spirited beast would be cheap at twice the price.

With its racy styling and immense speed, the Jota soon became a motorcycling status symbol.

Specification

(1976 model)

engine
Air-cooled, four-stroke, three-cylinder. 75mm (2.95 in.) bore X 74mm (2.91 in.) stroke = 980cc (60 cu.in.). Maximum power 90 bhp at 7600 rpm. Compression ratio 10:1. Two valves per cylinder operated directly by twin overhead camshafts. Three 32mm Dell'Orto carburetors

transmission
Five-speed gearbox. Chain drive

frame
Duplex cradle

suspension
Front - Ceriani telescopic fork
Rear - Swingarm with Ceriani coil-over shocks

brakes
Front - Twin Brembo discs
Rear - Single Brembo disc

weight
475 lbs. (216kg)

performance
Maximum speed 139 mph
Fuel consumption approximately 40 mpg

opposite Packed with power, this is the triple that drives the Jota.

above Peter Gibson hurls his Jota round Silverstone in 1976.

YAMAHA XS750

The Yamaha XS750, which marked Yamaha's entry into the sport touring market.

Honda started the superbike flood from Japan with the CB750 in 1969; Kawasaki followed suit with the Z1 in 1972. The success of those two indicated a public demand for more sophistication, and to many that meant four-cylinders. Later, the Honda Gold Wing seemed an even stronger indication. The two holdouts, Suzuki and Yamaha, continued in an entirely different vein, Suzuki with its GT750 triple and Yamaha with its small-bore two strokes.

In terms of displacement, Yamaha sported a 650cc vertical twin as top of its range, but the Triumph-like styling and vibration ensured the twin would remain more a cult machine. Yamaha's later TX750 and TX500 twins were notable for their complicated counterbalancing system, oil leaks, and an uncharacteristic lack of reliability. Neither could be termed a rousing success. Surely Yamaha would hedge its bets and produce something "safe," like a four-cylinder roadster.

In 1976 the answer was given: an emphatic, "*no.*" The new Yamaha was a transverse triple. At the time, the most significant feature of the XS750 was its shaft final drive, which distinctly said "touring" and marked the first time Yamaha had ventured into the realm of BMW and Moto Guzzi. Secondly, most manufacturers considered it practical to use shaft drive only with a longitudinal engine. Of course, MV Agusta had for many years been producing a transverse four with shaft drive, but how many people could afford an MV?

Here was an inexpensive bike with the sophistication and reliability expected from a Japanese machine, and added attraction of a clean, maintenance-free shaft drive. The original package was exceptionally neat, with a compact engine and transmission, alloy wheels, triple disc brakes, and subtle paintwork that made the bike seem even neater and smaller than it really was. And it didn't leak oil.

The XS750 features an almost "square" engine of 747cc, with dual overhead camshafts, three 34mm constant-vacuum carburetors and electronic ignition. With a compression ratio of 9.2:1, the engine produces 68 bhp at 7500 rpm and just under 50 lbs.ft. of torque. A wet, multi-plate clutch and five-speed gearbox put the power through a driveshaft in the left side of the swingarm. The gearchange is a bit notchier than most Japanese chain-drive bikes, but superior to most other "shafties."

The 750 features a rigid, duplex-cradle frame

Specification

(1978 model)

engine
Air-cooled, four-stroke, three-cylinder. 68mm (2.68 in.) bore X 68.6mm (2.7 in.) stroke = 747cc (46 cu.in.). Maximum power 68 bhp at 7500 rpm. Compression ratio 9.2:1. Two valves per cylinder operated directly by twin overhead camshafts. Three 34mm constant-vacuum Mikuni carburetors

transmission
Five-speed gearbox. Shaft drive

frame
Duplex cradle

suspension
Front - Kayaba telescopic fork
Rear - Swingarm with Kayaba coil-over shocks

brakes
Front - Twin Yamaha discs
Rear - Single Yamaha disc

weight
525 lbs. (238kg)

performance
Maximum speed 120 mph
Fuel consumption approximately 46 mpg

with a conventional suspension and triple discs on alloy wheels. Finish on the Yamaha is exemplary and the unique styling, complete with black engine cases, sets the bike apart from the crowd.

Starting the XS750 is easy regardless of weather, and the engine soon settles down to a burbling idle. The 120° crankshaft gives the XS a distinctive exhaust note, reminiscent of the Triumph Trident. With a quarter-mile time of 13.6 seconds, acceleration is some way off similar displacement fours, but top speed is just on 120 mph, only a few mph from its rivals. The XS750 is not designed as a sportster, however, and is much more at home when touring. This is emphasized by the handling, which is a little soft—to say the least—when it comes to scratching around country lanes.

The bike is more at home when loaded with a passenger and baggage and with a long journey ahead. Braking is something of a disappointment, but one tends to forget that the Yamaha belies its looks—it weighs more than 500 lbs. A firm grip on the lever is needed, but wet-weather braking is a pleasant surprise.

The original D and 2D models were somewhat soft on performance, but a later version of the bike, the XS750E, improved performance through a higher compression ratio, 9,000-rpm red line, and a few other modifications.

In 1979, the displacement was boosted to 850cc. Yamaha's advertising at the time boasted, "The Yamaha four-stroke philosophy: don't use more cylinders than you need." That's why they used three cylinders on the XS850? Maybe not, for a couple of months after that pronouncement, the XJ650 was introduced with a four-cylinder motor! Whatever, by this time the XS750 had a faithful following, if only of people who wanted something different.

Unloaded, the XS750 does not handle so well, but for touring it is certainly a good choice.

MV AGUSTA MONZA

The name of MV Agusta is a legend in motorcycling, for the company from Gallarate in northern Italy won 37 World Championships and more than 100 National titles. The Agusta concern, in fact, makes most of its money not from bikes, but by building Bell helicopters under license. Racing was something of a hobby for the company, and producing road bikes was even more so. Sadly, it now seems that the fire-engine-red racers and roadsters are no more; production ceased with the 750S America-based special.

The 837cc Monza was last produced in late 1978 and shared the production lines with the 861cc Arturo Magni special, which retailed for about 25 per cent more thanks to its extra performance parts. There was a vast amount of racing heritage in the last four-cylinder roadsters. Outwardly, it was hard to distinguish the production engines from those that powered the machines of Giacomo Agostini and Phil Read to several World Championships.

The basis of the Monza was a transverse-mounted, four-cylinder, twin-overhead-camshaft engine. The unit was sand-cast and looked rather unfinished by Japanese standards, but was still quite attractive. Inside, the unit differed from the racing engines in that it featured just two valves per cylinder and not four. It did, however, utilize the same precise and expensive gear drive for the overhead camshafts. The factory never disclosed power figures, but the Monza probably produced just over 75 bhp. More performance was available—at considerable expense—through a special four-valve head.

The whole engine unit was canted forward atop a five-speed gearbox and the drive turned 90° to a shaft drive. It was just about the sweetest changing and smoothest operating transmission of that type ever fitted to a motorcycle. If the weight penalty and power loss of a shaft drive could not be tolerated, the factory offered a chain-drive conversion. What made the bike stand out from the crowd was its sturdy duplex-cradle frame which, even if it did not resemble the racers too closely in looks, certainly gave the roadsters racer-type handling. Braking, too, was well up to standard with no less than three cast-iron discs, two at the front and one at the rear, stopping the 560-lb. bike easily in all weather.

The Monza was quite a compact bike and actually felt quite small to ride; the low seating position no doubt emphasized this impression. The growl through the four separate tailpipes recalled the racing heritage of the marque, and was wholly in keeping with the exceptionally fine road manners. High speeds were reached very quickly if the engine was kept near the 10,000-rpm redline. And high-speed cornering was effortless as the bike tending to stay absolutely planted, with the suspension and tires doing all the work.

Until recently, detail finish was never a strong point with Italian machines, but the MV was quite well finished with adequate, if not exceptional, instruments and switches.

It now seems that the bike side of the Agusta corporation is no more, and if that remains the case, the motorcycling world will be the poorer for it.

The MV Monza (opposite) was an easy bike to ride fast and felt very safe (below).

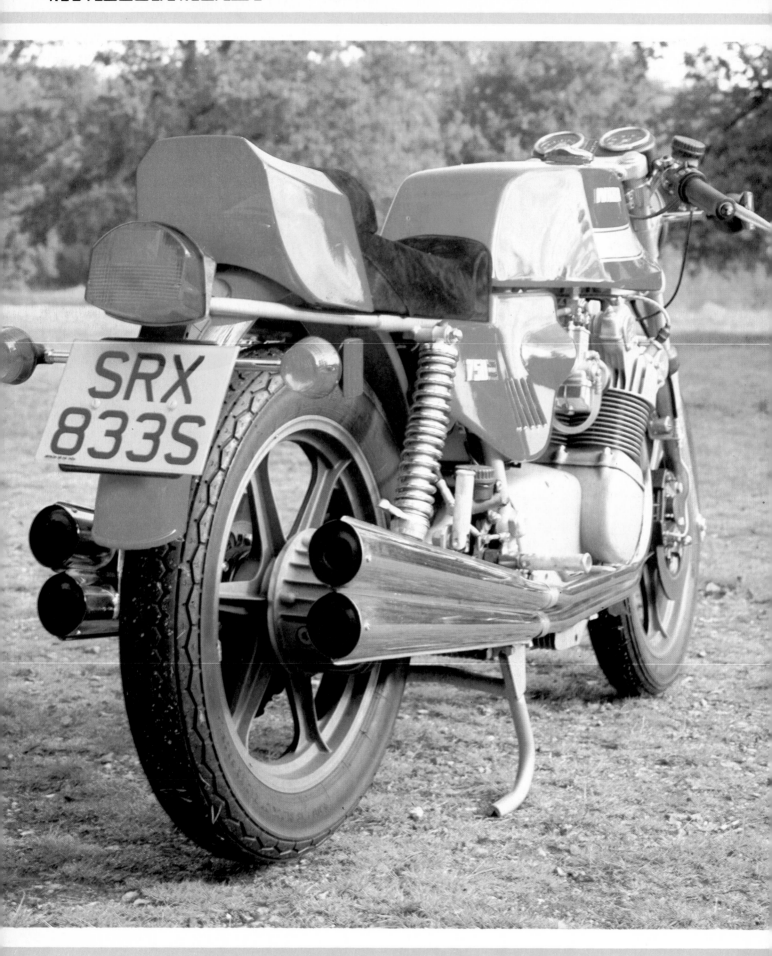

Specification

(1977 model)

engine
Air-cooled, four-stroke, four-cylinder. 69mm (2.72 in.) bore X 56mm (2.20 in.) stroke = 837cc (51 cu.in.). Maximum power 75 bhp at 9000 rpm. Compression ratio 9.3:1. Two valves per cylinder operated directly by twin overhead camshafts. Four 28mm Dell'Orto carburetors.

transmission
Five-speed gearbox.
Shaft drive

frame
Duplex cradle

suspension
Front - Ceriani telescopic fork
Rear - Swingarm with Ceriani coil-over shocks

brakes
Front - Twin Scarab discs
Rear - Single Scarab disc

weight
560 lbs. (254 kg)

performance
Maximum speed 140 mph
Fuel consumption approximately 40 mpg

opposite, above & left Various views of this very fast and well-finished superbike.

HARLEY-DAVIDSON XLCR1000

The cafe-racer Harley-Davidson XLCR of 1977.

The Harley-Davidson XLCR was unique in the range of models that roll from the Milwaukee factory; it was definitely not built on the same "laid back" lines as its stablemates. The CR part of the title stood for Cafe Racer, and the Harley was unquestionably one of the most aggressive-looking cafe racers available.

Although outwardly different from the other Harleys, the XLCR retained the Sportster V-twin. With very undersquare dimensions of 81mm X 96.8mm, the engine displaces 998cc. A 45° unit, the engine features a 9:1 compression ratio, pushrod-operated valves, and a single 38mm Keihin carburetor. Unsophisticated it may be, but the engine could pull a house down with its 61 bhp at 6200 rpm and, although undisclosed, probably around 60 lbs.ft. of torque. Although the torque figure is not quoted by the company, they do say that the "secret amount" occurs at 3500 rpm, well down the rev scale but just the thing for instant acceleration in any of the XLCR's four gears. An electric starter is the only concession to modern times, and it copes suprisingly well with getting the engine under way. Unlike a silky-smooth Japanese multi, there is no doubt when the Harley's engine is running. It has an off-beat exhaust note, it rumbles and shakes and leaves the rider in no doubt as to its capabilities.

Perhaps the most striking facet of the XLCR was the color—black, from the tinted screen to the mat-finish exhaust system. The engine, wet-multi-plate clutch and gearbox were mounted in a very narrow, duplex frame. The rear section and suspension were similar to the nearly unbeatable XR750 flat-track racers. Conventional springing was used, courtesy of Gabriel and Showa of Japan, with neat cast-aluminum wheels built by Morris. Kelsey-Hayes disc brakes were fitted, two front, one rear. Behind the bikini fairing were lowered bars, a 4.2-gallon fuel tank and a combined single-seat/rear-fairing.

When first astride the XLCR, one was aware that it was smaller than it looked. It weighed a trifling 485 lbs.—light by Harley standards—and was as slim as a pencil. This was complimented by the comfortable saddle, which was quite low—30.5 inches from the ground.

Once the carb had been primed with the throttle and the carburetor-mounted choke lever pulled out, the engine would fire immediately and settle down to a 900-rpm idle. The clutch was extraordinarily heavy and the gearchange vague, but once first had

been selected one could rocket away—the quarter mile took just over 13 seconds. There was really little point in taking the engine beyond 6000 rpm, and even changing gear at 4000 rpm allowed rapid progress. Vibration and a deafening roar were other reasons that made the approaching 6500-rpm redline of little value. The bike's top speed was really governed by low gearing, as the redline speed of just over 110 mph in top could be reached with no fuss at all.

With grippy Goodyear tires and a long wheelbase, the Harley handled well, with plenty of feel transmit-ted to the rider. In fact, on bumpy surfaces it would be fair to say the ride was "jarring," but that was worth it for a Harley that handled. Braking was "fair to middling" in the dry, but just about non-existent in the wet—waiting for the discs to work in the rain was hair-raising to say the least. On the other hand, the Goodyear A/T tires coped well with most conditions and the XLCR was a lot less of a handful than most of its stablemates when roads got wet and greasy.

Instrumentation was not up to the high standards set by the Japanese, as the two dials were quite

cheap-looking for such an expensive bike. The switches were worse than archaic. For instance, a simple button on either side of the bars worked the turn signals, but had to be depressed all the time the indicators were needed. Not exactly convenient when wrestling with the other controls.

In all, the Harley-Davidson did most things really well, with good acceleration, good handling, and crowd-pulling looks. Unfortunately, there was one thing it didn't do well—the bike never sold, and was dropped after two years.

Specification

(1977 model)

engine
Air-cooled, four-stroke, V-twin.
81mm (3.18 in.) bore
X 96.8mm (3.81 in.) stroke
= 998cc (61 cu.in.). Maximum power
61 bhp at 6200 rpm. Compression
ratio 9:1. Two valves per cylinder
operated via pushrods and rockers
by four individual camshafts. Single
38mm Keihin carburetor

transmission
Four-speed gearbox. Chain drive

frame
Duplex cradle

suspension
Front - Showa telescopic forks
Rear - Swingarm with Gabriel coil-
over shocks

brakes
Front - Twin Kelsey-Hayes discs
Rear - Single Kelsey-Hayes disc

weight
485 lbs. (220kg)

performance
Maximum speed 111 mph
Fuel consumption approximately
49 mpg

With its nearly all-black look, the XLCR was a real crowd puller.

inset The 4.2 gallon fuel tank, with the old-style Harley-Davidson badge, and the air filter cover directly below it.

SEELEY HONDA 750

The old adage "racing improves the breed" was perhaps never more true than in the case of the Seeley Honda 750. Although the Seeley is not a racing bike, its manufacturer, Colin Seeley, has spent his whole life involved with racing motorcycles. Seeley himself was British sidecar-racing champion and his whole outlook on motorcycling is steeped in the racing tradition.

The Seeley Honda is an attempt to combine the best aspects of both the British and Japanese motorcycle industries. The British are acknowledged aces at building frames, while the Japanese are likewise when it comes to designing sophisticated, yet reliable engines. Put the two together, reasoned Colin Seeley, and you have the ultimate motorcycle.

For the frame, Seeley designed an exceptionally strong duplex cradle using Reynolds 531 tubing. The workmanship is a joy to behold; all joints are hand fitted before brazing. Not only is the frame stronger, it is 25 lbs. lighter than the stock Honda CB750 frame.

The engine is Honda's tried and trusted single-overhead-camshaft motor, but plans are being made to redesign the frame to accommodate the

later twin-cam version. The original 736cc engine pushes out a respectable 67 bhp and has proven itself over the years to be a smooth and practically unbreakable unit. It has plenty of torque for smooth takeoffs and easy riding.

The Honda engine is representative of Seeley's attitude toward sophistication—it does not necessarily mean "exotic." Stock parts are replaced only if a genuine improvement can be made, and not at the expense of reliability. The electrical system is stock and the slick five-speed gearbox is also unchanged. The one questionable component is the stock Honda front fork. Otherwise, where an improvement can be made it is. The Seeley frame and Honda engine are complimented by a variety of other first-rate pieces: Lockheed brakes, Lester wheels, and Girling rear shocks.

The appearance of the machine is enhanced by a sleek 5.5-gallon tank, a natty little windshield and a racy, single-place seat. The Seeley looks like 100 mph standing still.

The Seeley Honda 750 is in its element out on the open road. The combination of a stiff, strong chassis and a smooth, powerful, civilized engine ensures that the bike is a pleasure to ride. Handling and steering are first-rate, and corners can be taken at quite breathtaking speeds. The grippy Avon tires, mounted on their attractive Lester cast-aluminum wheels, also make for good roadholding. Directional changes can be made with a minimum of fuss and, together with the bike's powerful brakes, the Seeley inspires great confidence.

The machine is not without its faults, however. The bike is fitted with a small and rather hard seat, so after a few hours in action it begins to make its presence felt. The other major complaint is with the Honda front forks. Never shining examples of suspension technology, they are somewhat harsh and will flex under fierce braking or cornering loads. Bear in mind, however, that this complaint can only be made when the bike is being ridden in a manner that would land you in jail. It is possible to have other forks fitted but, of course, this can be an expensive business. Seeley has chosen the stock

Part of the Seeley Honda's British-built frame.

units simply because of their cost factor and, if nothing else, the Seeley Honda is certainly one of the more reasonably priced superbike specials.

Because the Seeley uses the stock Honda motor, fuel consumption is quite reasonable. In standard form the Seeley should return about 40 miles to the gallon. Of course, you can bore the engine out to 1000cc, fit all sorts of go-fast goodies and create yourself a real fire-eater. Your wallet might not be able to take it, but it is odds-on that Seeley's frame can. And there aren't too many bikes around about which that can be said.

The 1978 Seeley Honda with its 750cc Honda engine.

Specification

engine
Air-cooled, four-stroke, four-cylinder. 61mm (2.40 in.) bore X 63mm (2.48 in.) stroke = 736cc (45 cu.in.). Maximum power 67 bhp at 8500 rpm. Compression ratio 9.2:1. Two valves per cylinder operated via rockers by a single overhead camshaft. Four

28mm Keihin carburetors
transmission
Five-speed gearbox.
Chain drive
frame
Duplex cradle
suspension
Front - Showa (Honda) telescopic fork
Rear - Swingarm with Girling

coil-over shocks
brakes
Front - Twin Lockheed discs
Rear - Single Lockheed disc
weight
499 lbs. (227kg)
performance
Maximum speed 120 mph
Fuel consumption approximately 43 mpg

YAMAHA XS1100

Nobody could accuse the Boeing 747 Jumbo Jet of being a lively performer in the air, yet, as anyone who has ever traveled on a 747 will testify, the big plane's take-off is a breathtakingly impressive business.

It would not be unfair to call the Yamaha XS1100 the Boeing 747 of motorcycling. It is a big, heavy machine with a turbine-smooth ride—just made for carrying rider and passenger long distances with a minimum of fuss. It also has rocket-like acceleration. Open the throttle and the XS disappears into the distance with that same smooth, deceptively powerful push-in-the-seat that so distinguishes the 747.

The Yamaha XS1100 first made its appearance around the end of 1977 and went on sale a few months later. It is Yamaha's answer to the glut of superbikes that made their appearance around the same time, bikes like the Honda CBX, Suzuki GS1000 and Kawasaki Z1R. It soon became obvious, however, that the XS wasn't aimed at quite the same market as a bike like the Z1R, which is virtually an out-and-out straight-line racer. Not that the XS1100 isn't an impressive straight-line performer itself—a quarter-mile time of 12.3 seconds is quick in anyone's language. But its sheer size and weight—620-plus lbs. fully laden—coupled with its

shaft drive, put it straight into the heavyweight touring market, where it has few peers.

The heart of the XS1100 is a four-stroke, four-cylinder, 1101cc, twin-overhead-cam engine developing a massive 95 bhp at 8000 rpm, sufficient to propel the beast to a top speed of almost 135 mph. It breathes through four 34mm constant-vacuum Mikuni carburetors and produces an awesome 66 lbs.ft. of torque at 6500 rpm, giving more mid-range punch than almost any other motorcycle engine on the market.

The Yamaha's introduction, however, was greeted with some mixed feelings. The XS1100 is certainly impressive to ride, but its steering and handling leave a bit to be desired. The supple suspension that does so well on "autopilot" is quickly overworked during back-road maneuvers. With so much power on tap and so much weight, the XS doesn't care too much for swift directional changes, and many a road tester has returned to base wide-eyed and white-faced after the beast failed to do exactly what was required. Insurance companies tend to look the other way when asked for coverage quotes; the prospective buyer needs to be fairly serious about his motorcycling before laying out his cash.

Nevertheless, the XS1100 has found a niche. It's become a great favorite with long-distance riders, particularly in the US The smooth ride and wide, comfortable seat make it a most pleasant machine to ride over long distances. With a sensible 5.3-gallon fuel tank and an overall consumption around 40 mpg, the XS1100 also has a good fuel range, a vital asset to the serious tourer. In addition, it has a host of luxuries as standard equipment. These include self-cancelling turn signals, a fuel gauge, adjustable forks and dampers, and an emergency engine switch which kills the engine if the bike is ever cranked over more than 60°—i.e., if you ever throw it away. Finally, of course, it is big enough to carry the big fairings and saddlebags, so beloved of many long-distance tourers.

Yamaha XS1100 fans will probably object to their bike being compared to a 747 Jumbo Jet, but no disrespect is intended. Both machines were created for a specific purpose and both perform their duties in dramatic fashion. Even the most jaded of travelers could not fail to be impressed by that astonishingly powerful, yet velvet-smooth takeoff.

The instrument layout on the XS1 includes a fuel gauge.

The smooth-riding, shaft-driven 1979 XS1100.

Specification

(1978 model)

engine
Air-cooled, four-stroke, four-cylinder.
71.5mm (2.81 in.) bore X 68.6mm (2.70 in.) stroke = 1102cc (68 cu.in.). Maximum power 95 bhp at 8000 rpm. Compression ratio 9.2:1. Two valves per cylinder operated directly by twin overhead camshafts. Four 34mm Mikuni constant-vacuum carburetors

transmission
Five-speed gearbox.
Shaft drive

frame
Duplex cradle

suspension
Front - Kayaba telescopic fork
Rear - Swingarm with Kayaba coil-over shocks

brakes
Front - Twin Yamaha discs
Rear - Single Yamaha disc

weight
564 lbs. (256kg)

performance
Maximum speed 134mph
Fuel consumption approximately 40 mpg

TRIUMPH BONNEVILLE

When Edward Turner was pencilling his design for the Triumph Speed Twin way back in the mid-'30s, he could scarcely have dreamed that the same basic design would be used to power a superbike of the '70s, the Triumph Bonneville.

The Bonneville is something of an anachronism in the world of motorcycling, but much of its success is due to its absolute simplicity. With a pushrod ver-

The engine of the 750 Bonneville, the basic design of which dates back to the 1930s.

tical-twin engine, the Bonneville offers an alternative to a world dominated by multi-cylinder machines. It is about 100 lbs. lighter than most of its Japanese rivals, and with a crankcase measuring about 14 inches across, it is a good eight inches narrower than the average Japanese four. The light weight and slim build also mean the bike's maneuverability and handling are far superior to most of its rivals.

Powerplant of the Bonneville is a straightforward piece of machinery. Two cylinders, each measuring 76mm X 82mm, give a total capacity of 744cc, while the valves are operated by pushrods. Two Amal carburetors provide fuel for the 8.6:1 compression motor, giving a power output of 49 bhp at 6200 rpm, not a great deal by modern standards. The engine does, however, offer usable torque even at the lowest revs.

The most serious problem surrounding the Bonneville is the classic one common to most vertical twins—vibration. At high revs the bike vibrates quite severely, sending tingling sensations through the rider's arms and shoulders which at times may even become painful.

Another criticism levelled at the Bonneville is that it leaks oil. Today's models, however, are a far cry from the old non-unit models of the '50s and are, by comparison, oil-tight.

Visually, the Bonneville has changed little over the years. It still retains the lean and lithe look that is so typically British and made it so popular over the years. The paint finish on the tank, much of it hand applied at the factory, is superb. The bike is immaculately finished, proof of the loving care and attention that goes into the building of these machines.

The Bonneville may not have the performance or sophistication of its multi-cylinder rivals but it does have something that most of them lack—an almost human personality, maddeningly idiosyncratic, occasionally unreliable but invariably friendly.

Originally the Bonneville was a 650cc bike. This 1978 model is 750cc and has American styling.

Specification

(1978 model)

engine
Air-cooled, four-stroke, twin-cylinder. 76mm (2.99 in.) bore X 82mm (3.23 in.) stroke = 744cc (46 cu.in.). Maximum power 49 bhp at 6200 rpm. Compression ratio 8.6:1. Two valves per cylinder operated via pushrods and rockers by twin camshafts. Two 30mm

Amal carburetors
transmission
Five-speed gearbox.
Chain drive
frame
Duplex cradle
suspension
Front - Triumph telescopic fork
Rear - Swingarm with Girling coil-over shocks

brakes
Front - Single Lockheed disc
Rear - Single Lockheed disc
weight
395 lbs. (179kg)
performance
Maximum speed 108 mph
Fuel consumption approximately 45 mpg

HONDA CBX

By the late '70s, the Japanese motorcycle industry had grown so strong that the major Japanese companies could allow themselves the luxury of indulging in a little muscle flexing. Honda, Kawasaki, Yamaha and Suzuki all introduced bikes with staggering power capabilities, and 1/4-mile acceleration became the major criterion for judging superbike performance. At its introduction in 1978, the most outrageous of all was Honda's CBX.

The CBX is a *tour de force* of Honda technology, but the engine is the most impressive piece. Its specifications read like those of a four-stroke GP machine: six cylinders, dual overhead cams, four valves per cylinder, six 28mm carburetors, 10,500 rpm. A power output of 105 bhp at 9000 rpm gives the big machine—and it is big—a top speed over 130 mph. To this technological extravagance Honda adds a five-speed gearbox, chain final drive, three disc brakes, Comstar wheels, tubeless tires and every electrical gadget it can justify.

Suddenly, anyone with enough money—and the CBX is most reasonably priced—can purchase a motorcycle offering the kind of performance that ten years before would have been available only on a Grand Prix racer. One problem with the CBX, however, is that it isn't a Grand Prix racer. At 555 lbs., the CBX is a very heavy machine and even though the frame—which uses the engine as a stressed member—is an improvement over the majority of Japanese sport machines, it certainly cannot be thrown around like a lightweight. And the ride is deceptively smooth, a potential danger to any inexperienced rider.

Another problem with the CBX is its maintenance cost. Dealer servicing is recommended every 3750 miles and only the most expert owner would contemplate doing his own service. And, the chain and rear tire need replacement every 4000 miles, making the CBX an expensive proposition to run.

For most owners, however, the disadvantages are outweighed by the sheer prestige and enjoyment of owning and riding such a machine. With its spectacular acceleration—a quarter mile under 12 seconds is normal—the CBX is an exhilarating bike to ride. Its velvet smoothness also makes even the longest journey a pleasure. Also, as a status symbol and head turner the CBX has few equals in the motorcycling world—many a CBX has been sold for that reason alone.

The road-going 1979 CBX.

The CBX of Monin Louis and Laurens Thierry, prior to the start of the 1979 Bol d'Or endurance race at the Paul Ricard circuit in the south of France.

above The first CBX on a European strip ran at Santa Pod and clocked a time of 11.7 seconds.

opposite 105 bhp, twin overhead camshafts, six cylinders, this is the *pièce de résistance* of the CBX.

Specification

(1978 model)

engine
Air-cooled, four-stroke, six-cylinder. 64.5mm (2.54 in.) bore X 53.4mm (2.10 in.) stroke = 1047cc (64 cu.in.). Maximum power 105 bhp at 9000 rpm. Compression ratio 9.3:1. Four valves per cylinder operated directly by twin overhead camshafts. Six 28mm Keihin constant-vacuum carburetors

transmission
Five-speed gearbox. Chain drive

frame
Diamond-type backbone.

suspension
Front - Showa telescopic fork
Rear - Swingarm with adjustable Showa FVQ coil-over shocks

brakes
Front - Twin Honda discs
Rear - Single Honda disc

weight
548 lbs. (249kg)

performance
Maximum speed 136 mph
Fuel consumption approximately 33 mpg

KAWASAKI KZ1300

With bikes like the H1 500, the H2 750 and the Z-1, Kawasaki earned a reputation for making the fastest and the most fearsome machines available. But as the '70s wore on, the opposition began to catch up with their own scorching road burners. Since 1973, however, Kawasaki Heavy Industries had been working on a new "King" to guarantee their position in motorcycling's heirarchy.

The brief was simple: a 1200cc, six-cylinder, inline engine. Development continued on those lines until it was decided that, due to the bike's inevitable weight penalty, an even larger power unit was necessary. When the KZ1300 was finally announced to the press in late 1978, it featured a 1286cc engine.

The width of a six-cylinder, transverse-mounted power unit presents the biggest problem for designers because it limits cornering clearance. Such a unit also has a large frontal area, which increases aerodynamic drag and makes maneuvering in traffic somewhat perilous.

Kawasaki's answer to the problem of making a compact six was water cooling. Without the need for cooling fins around each cylinder, the bore-center distance can be reduced. Of course, another

opposite Power for the Kawasaki KZ1300 is transmitted via a five-speed gearbox to a shaft on the right side of the bike.

below Easy-to-read instrumentation on the KZ1300.

advantage of water cooling is good sound insulation; consequently, this well-balanced six is notably quiet and smooth. Engine width also partially accounts for the decidely undersquare dimensions of the engine. For a given displacement, a small bore/long stroke allows tighter bore spacing than an oversquare engine.

The customary one carburetor per cylinder would have severely limited rider position, so the decision was made to use three two-barrel, constant-vacuum carburetors and long angled-inlet runners. The compact carburetors are under the fuel tank where they won't impose on the rider. Fuel/air mixture enters the combustion chamber through a single valve, the company thinking the expense and complexity of the four-valve-per-cylinder system was unnecessary. Power output proves them right.

Power is transmitted through a jackshaft behind the cylinders, then through a five-speed gearbox to a drive shaft mounted on the right side of the bike. With 640 lbs. to propel and 120 bhp to transmit to the 17-in rear wheel, it was obvious that a chain would not be up to the job. Braking is taken care of by triple discs with sintered-metal pads.

Surprisingly, once under way the bike is quite easy to ride. There is no noticeable peakiness, just one turbine-like surge right up to the 8000-rpm mark. This corresponds to 135 mph in top gear, although a few more mph can be extracted if you risk running past redline. Acceleration is certainly in the top bracket, with a quarter-mile time just reaching into the "elevens." There are one or two bikes which are faster, but they are considerably lighter and not quite so comfortable. Another pleasant surprise is the machine's fuel consumption, which is always on the good side of 40 mpg.

The instrumentation and switchgear of the bike are just what you would expect of a Japanese bike for the 1980s—just about perfect. The KZ1300 has a large, comfortable saddle which makes long-distance touring very comfortable indeed.

Although it appears that the trend toward "bigger is better" has leveled off, critics should not dismiss the KZ1300 as the ultimate unmanageable monster. It is in fact smooth, fast, easy to ride and an interesting step in the development of the superbike.

above The seat lock is neatly tucked way in the side panel.

right The complete KZ1300, which Kawasaki believed would be the superbike to beat all superbikes.

Specification

(1979 model)

engine
Water-cooled, four-stroke, six-cylinder. 62mm (2.44 in.) bore X 71mm (2.80 in.) stroke = 1286cc (78 cu.in.). Maximum power 120 bhp at 8000 rpm. Compression ratio 9.9:1. Two valves per cylinder operated directly by twin overhead camshafts. Three two-barrel 32mm Mikuni constant-vacuum carburetors

transmission
Five-speed gearbox. Shaft drive

frame
Duplex cradle

suspension
Front - Kayaba telescopic fork
Rear - Swingarm with Kayaba coil-over shocks

brakes
Front - Twin Kawasaki discs
Rear - Single Kawasaki disc

weight
684 lbs. (310kg)

performance
Maximum speed 135 mph
Fuel consumption approximately 44 mpg

HONDA CB900FZ

With a superbly set-up frame, the CB900FZ has remarkably good handling characteristics.

Manufacturers often claim a direct connection between their street machines and their racing hardware, but often the similarity amounts to little more than the number of wheels. One notable exception is the Honda CB900FZ, or Bol d'Or as it's known in Europe. If its specifications seem a little familiar, that's due to its racing parentage, the one-liter Honda wonders that have been cleaning up in endurance racing for the past few years.

The 900's evolution is not just a simple matter of racer turned road-burner, however. In fact, it goes back to the time when Honda was looking for a new sports flagship. With vast funds available for research and development Honda R & D had free rein to develop whatever model they thought fit.

Under the watchful eye of Soichiro Irimajiri, renowned for his racing bikes of the '60s and for his hand in the company's Formula One car projects, two bikes were developed. Both machines were of one-liter capacity, both had approximately the same straight-line performance, and both used lots of Honda's racing expertise. The only difference between the two models was the number of cylinders; one was a conventional four, the other, a six. The six was a shade quicker than the four, sounded different and, most importantly, looked different. It, of course, became the CBX.

Honda, however, had other plans for the one-liter four. With engine size reduced to 902cc, it was marketed as the CB900FZ. The bike follows the style of the twin-cam versions of the 750, but its engine has more in common with the six-cylinder CBX. They share the same 64.5mm bore, but the 900 has a 15.4mm longer stroke. Its stroke is actually 69mm, making the unit undersquare—quite a rarity on a modern motorcycle engine. With a compression ratio of 8.8:1 the 900 produces a staggering 95 bhp at 9000 rpm. This, no doubt, is due to the motor's efficient breathing by way of four 32mm carburetors and four valves per cylinder.

The rest of the mix in the CB900FZ package is quite straightforward, with a wet, multi-plate clutch, five-speed gearbox, chain drive, duplex-cradle frame, conventional swingarm suspenion, and triple discs. The package also includes Honda's unique Comstar wheels, which are fabricated from a number of spun- and cast-aluminum pieces.

What the specifications don't reflect is that the bike has one of the best chassis available from the Orient—far superior to the Irimajiri-inspired dia-

mond-spine frame of the CBX. In handling, the CB900FZ is a revelation. It feels just like an Italian superbike, and that really is high praise indeed. Only at the far end of the speed scale are its manners anything less than superb.

The CB900FZ is a shatteringly fast motorcycle. It has a top speed above 130 mph, and the roads where that speed is attainable are few and far between. Just as impressive is the 900's quarter-mile time of 12.3 seconds, putting it on a par with Kawasaki's KZ1000 and Suzuki's GS1000, both machines sporting engines larger than the Honda's.

In spite of its rocket-like performance, the CB900FZ is highly refined, with silky-smooth manners and the feel of a true thoroughbred. Its braking is excellent.

The CB900FZ may be slightly slower than its big brother, the CBX, but it has two assets the big six-cylinder machine lacks. Not only is the 900's handling definitely superior to the that of the CBX's, but the CB900FZ is surprisingly economical, returning 40 mpg.

It may seem that with the FZ and the CBX Honda has turned out overlapping models. It is not until one has ridden both bikes that the differences are

No more dials and switches than necessary are used on the instrument panel (right) and left handlebar (below), which includes an easy-to-operate choke lever.

obvious and noteworthy. Unless ridden full bore, there is little contrast. But when the upper realms are reached, the CB900FZ's fine chassis puts it above the CBX, while the CBX has an engine that is second to none. As Mark Twain once explained: "You pays your money and takes your choices."

The FZ engine provides
very quick acceleration as
well as an impressive top
speed.

Specification

(1979 model)

engine
Air-cooled, four-stroke, four-cylinder. 64.5mm (2.63 in.) bore X 69mm (2.72 in.) stroke = 902cc (55 cu.in.). Maximum power 95 bhp at 9000 rpm. Compression ratio 8.8:1. Four valves per cylinder operated directly by twin overhead camshafts. Four 32mm Keihin constant-vacuum carburetors

transmission
Five-speed gearbox.
Chain drive
frame
Duplex cradle
suspension
Front - Showa telescopic fork
Rear - Swingarm with Showa
FVQ coil-over shocks
brakes
Front - Twin Honda discs

Rear - Single Honda disc
weight
510 lbs. (232kg)
performance
Maximum speed 132mph
Fuel consumption
approximately 41 mpg

RICKMAN KAWASAKI CRE

Just as there seems to be something in Italy that enables its manufacturers to produce some of the world's most exotic machines, there's something about England—the tea, perhaps—that enables the English to produce some of the world's best frames.

Among the best of the British frame-makers are the Rickman brothers, Don and Derek, who operate from a small factory in Hampshire. Having gained fame building motocrossers, they turned their attention to road machines. In early 1974 they introduced a rolling chassis for the four-cylinder Honda CB750 engine. In its original guise as a cafe-racer, the Rickman CR had few faults, and its handling was a vast improvement over the stock Honda's. In time, further modifications were made to the frame, and the more powerful four-cylinder Kawasaki Z-1 engine was slotted into the chassis. The Rickman

brothers then decided to take the concept one step further with their CRE Endurance model. This differed from the original CR models in that the Endurance version came clothed in a fully stream-lined fairing, modeled after those used for long-distance racing events such as the Bol d'Or.

The CRE utilized the standard Rickman frame, a duplex cradle built of the tried and trusted Reynolds 531 chrome-moly tubing, then nickel-plated after construction. The workmanship that goes into building the frame is of the highest quality. Unfortunately, a few days in the elements will tarnish its nickel-plating, and only great care will keep it looking good.

The bike itself is very attractive, with the sleek rounded fairing and twin headlights giving it a rakish appearance. A streamlined tail section is also incorporated, so the CRE is sure to turn heads wherever it goes. The fairing is both attractive and practical as it allows the rider to crouch behind it almost completely protected from the elements.

The CRE's power unit is the ubiquitous Kawasaki KZ1000 four-cylinder, known for its bullet-proof dependability. The latest version of this twin-over-head-camshaft engine punches out 93 bhp, enough to give the CRE a top speed above 130 mph. The standard five-speed Kawasaki gearbox is retained, but the final-drive ratio can be altered to cater to the aspirations of CRE owners. The engine itself has plenty of torque and is exceptionally flexible. Fuel consumption is another asset of the CRE, as the big Kawasaki engine uses only one gallon of gas every 45 miles.

The CRE's handling is impressive. Pirelli Phantom tires provide excellent grip and the sturdy frame ensures safe and stable cornering. Combine this with the Spanish Betor front forks and "flat-out" riding becomes an exhilarating experience. The bike can be leaned to angles that would send many a stock machine cartwheeling down the road, and directional changes can be made swiftly with just a flick of the wrists. The suspension is taut and firm, but not too harsh, and the riding position is well tailored for high-speed work. All in all, the CRE conveys to its rider a sense of confidence and competence that many so-called superbikes totally lack.

But the CRE does have its drawbacks. The fairing

right The sleek, rounded fairing of the CRE with its twin headlamps.

opposite The unusual look of the CRE is sure to turn heads wherever it goes.

The streamlined tail
section of the CRE.

Standard Kawasaki dials and warning lights are used on the CRE.

Specification

engine
Air-cooled, four-stroke, four-cylinder. 70mm (2.75 in.) bore X 66mm (2.6 in.) stroke = 1015cc (62 cu.in.). Maximum power 93 bhp at 8000 rpm. Compression ratio 8.7:1. Two valves per cylinder operated directly by twin overhead camshafts. Four 28mm Mikuni carburetors

transmission
Five-speed gearbox. Chain drive

frame
Duplex cradle

suspension
Front - Betor telescopic fork
Rear - Swingarm with Girling coil-over shocks

brakes
Front - Twin Lockheed discs
Rear - Single Lockheed disc

weight
510 lbs. (231kg)

performance
Maximum speed 132 mph
Fuel consumption approx 45 mpg

tends to hamper the rider in heavy, slow-moving traffic. And although it has a dual seat, the position of the rear footpegs and an unusually sloped seat makes two-up riding an unhappy proposition. Riding the CRE is best practiced alone.

These shortcomings, however, are relatively unimportant when measured against the CRE's remarkable abilities. For sheer riding pleasure the CRE is hard to beat.

BIMOTA KAWASAKI KB1

The 138 mph KB1.

Massimo Tamburini decided to revamp his MV-Agusta 600 back in 1970. This enthusiast from Rimini scrapped the bike's original frame and substituted one of his own manufacture. He uprated the engine, then made his own chain final drive to replace the MV's shaft system. So enthusiastic were press reports when the bike was unveiled that Massimo soon had people begging him to manufacture rolling chassis for their engines. Thirty lucky Honda 750 owners were the first to benefit from the engineer's skills, and when they announced they were more than happy with their bikes, Massimo decided to close down his plumbing business and set up a bike factory.

His factory not only produces rolling chassis, but racing models too. Eventually, the Bimota company's frames sheathed the works Yamaha of John Cecotto and the GP Harley-Davidson of Walter Villa, who took a total of four World Championships between them.

The first series-production bike built by the three directors of the company, *BI*anchi, *MO*rri and *TA*mburini, is one which is still in production, the KB1. Although quite straightforward in design compared to the later SB2 and SB3 models, the Kawasaki-based Bimota is still miles ahead of most other "cafe-racers."

The KB1 stands out as one of the most purposeful and neatly constructed chassis in motorcycling. Attractively finished in bright red, the chrome-moly frame uses the engine as a stressed member. Critical areas, like the steering head and swing-arm pivot, are heavily braced for extra rigidity. A cantilever rear end is used, with a single, horizontal Corte and Cosso coil-over shock. Brembo calipers and cross-drilled, cast-iron discs are fitted to the bike's Campagnolo magnesium wheels. Instruments and switchgear are standard Kawasaki.

The machine is finished off with tank and bodywork almost identical to that of the 1977 works Yamahas, which were noted for being particularly attractive and aerodynamically efficient. Obviously, with a low-set riding position and the aid of a fairing—not to mention the weight saving of almost 100 lbs.—the KB1 is both faster and quicker than the standard Kawasaki. The bike rockets away from the start right up to its maximum speed of 138 mph in almost no time at all. Top speed is governed by the gearing, but longer-legged gears would blunt

the bike's acceleration, and acceleration is one of its main attractions.

Obviously, the Bimota's other attraction is its road manners, which are simply impeccable. The KB1 is a bike that would be quite at home on a race track, and this is brought home when the first bend is encountered. The bike just begs to be banked hard into corners at seemingly impossible speeds, and it rewards the rider with handling as secure as can be expected on two wheels. The ride is firm without being harsh, and the suspension is very well damped. Scraping any part of the bike in turns—

without throwing the bike away—is nearly impossible on public roads, and rarely done on a race track. Put simply, the KB1's abilities are above and beyond those of most of its riders. Braking, too, is of the highest order under all conditions—just as you would expect.

There have been a few minor changes on the KB1 since its introduction, primarily to make the bike more civilized. The first KB1s were a little unwieldy in traffic due to insufficient steering lock, but later models have large indentations in the upper frame tubes behind the steering head to allow for more

Specification

engine
Air-cooled, four-stroke, four-cylinder. 70mm (2.75 in.) bore X 66mm (2.6 in.) stroke = 1015cc (62 cu.in.). Maximum power 93 bhp at 8000 rpm. Compression ratio 8.7:1. Two valves per cylinder operated directly by twin overhead camshafts. Four 28mm Mikuni carburetors

transmission
Five-speed gearbox.
Chain drive

frame
Multi-tubular backbone, stressed engine

suspension
Front - Marzocchi telescopic fork
Rear - Cantilever monoshock with Corte and Cosso coil-over shock

brakes
Front - Twin Brembo discs
Rear - Single Brembo disc

weight
418 lbs. (190kg)

performance
Maximum speed 138 mph
Fuel consumption approximately 76 mpg

movement. They look a bit crude and may seem a grotesque compromise, but seem to have little effect on frame rigidity. Another concession to civility is the seating. The latest KB1's tail fairing/saddle can be unclipped and replaced by a twin-seat unit. Passenger pegs are located in the rear bodywork. Of course, the passenger may be uncomfortable, but the pleasures of Bimota travel are worth a little suffering.

The Bimota frame is made from chrome-moly tubing and finished in bright red.

SUZUKI GSX1100

By the late '70s, the world seemed to be closing in on the superbikes. Germany was the first to impose a ban on all motorcycles with more than 100 bhp, soon after the launch of the 120 bhp Kawasaki KZ1300. Kawasaki quickly responded with a restricted version of their flagship. Honda was the next to comply with the regulations; the CBX lost 10 of its 105 bhp in the 1979-1980 transition.

At the time, Suzuki was preparing an 1100cc model of its 90 bhp GS1000. With 10 percent more capacity than its earlier stablemate, and a brand new four-valve head, it seemed obvious it should have much more power. But this was in fact not the case, for the new GS1100 had a fraction under the permitted 100 bhp. Yet it could still outperform every other production motorcycle in the world.

A whole new wave of technology has washed over the basic two-valve Suzuki engine to produce the GS1100 TSCC (Twin Swirl Combustion Chamber) motor. Despite the apparent marketing-embellished engineerese, there's more to it than a title. Apart from the obvious doubling of valves, the engine features nearly square combustion chambers and an exceedingly complex combustion chamber designed to encourage swirl. Smaller intake ports increase the fuel/air-mixture velocity,

right The instrument cluster used on the 1978 GS1000.

opposite The GS1000S did not differ much from its predecessor, the GS1000.

and the resulting turbulence improves distribution throughout the combustion chamber.

Interestingly the one potential advantage of having four valves per cylinder—greater valve area—has not been exploited. The 1100 has a total 38mm^2 more valve area per cylinder than the 1000. This represents a valve-area increase of less than 2%, despite an actual 8% increase in displacement. While the difference could be overcome through more radical camshaft timing, the GS1100 actually has a milder cam than the non-TSCC GS1000. Suzuki states that at lower valve openings, the multi-valve head is far more efficient, and all the figures bear them out. Despite its horsepower output, the engine is economical at 42—48 mpg. A CBX, by comparison, does well to hit 35 mpg.

A normal duplex-cradle frame is used for the GS, in conjunction with air forks. With the 1100, Suzuki finally fitted a balance pipe between the two fork legs, so equal pressure is assured in both. Although the air pressure can be adjusted, Suzuki recommends 7.1 psi; no more, no less. The rest of the adjustments, however, should be enough to satisfy the most avid fiddler. There are four spring-preload and four rebound-damping adjustments at the front, and four rebound settings and five preload settings at the rear. It's all something of a nightmare for the novice, but a dream come true for the road-going racer who takes great delight in setting up his bike for every conceivable road condition and style of riding.

Weighing just 535 lbs., considerably less than its rivals, and with nearly 100 bhp on tap, the Suzuki flagship is quite a road burner. In fact, its 11.5-second quarter-mile time suggests that if anything, the quoted power figures are a little on the conservative side. Apart from the shattering acceleration and the gearing-governed top speed of 141 mph, the bike pulls like a train without the occasional mid-range flat spot found on the 1000. Handling is excellent, even better than on previous Suzuki models. In short, it rates with just about any other bike on the market.

Far from being a slightly modified GS1000, the GS1100 Suzuki really deserves to be rated as a completely new bike. It is the lightest, quickest, fastest and most frugal in its class, and it handles every bit as well if not better than its rivals. What more could one want?

Specification

(1980 model)

engine
Air-cooled, four-stroke, four-cylinder.
72mm (2.83 in.) bore
X 66mm (2.60 in.) stroke
= 1075cc (66 cu.in.). Maximum
power 98 bhp at 8700 rpm.
Compression ratio 9.5:1. Four valves
per cylinder operated via stub
rockers by twin overhead camshafts.
Four 34mm Mikuni constant-vacuum
carburetors

transmission
Five-speed gearbox. Chain drive

frame
Duplex cradle

suspension
Front - Kayaba telescopic air fork
Rear - Swingarm with Kayaba
adjustable coil-over shocks

brakes
Front - Twin Suzuki discs
Rear - Single Suzuki disc

weight
535 lbs. (243kg)

performance
Maximum speed 141 mph
Fuel consumption approximately
45 mpg

top   The much revised instrument panel of the 1980 GSX1100.

right   A square headlamp is another new feature of the GSX.

HONDA GOLD WING

For many years the availability of purpose-built touring motorcycles was limited, with available hardware either too expensive or unreliable. In 1974 Honda remedied the situation with the GL1000 Gold Wing. Proclaimed the "ultimate" in touring machines, the original Gold Wing was whisper-quiet, water-cooled, shaft-driven and smooth. Performance was also admirable. The flat-four engine, giving the bike a top speed near 125 mph, made the GL1000 an easy match for many of the best "sports" machines around. Only its weight and suspension gave rise to criticism.

But the Gold Wing engine has always been considered an engineering masterpiece. At the front of each cylinder-bank, a single overhead camshaft is driven by a toothed rubber belt. This makes for a very quiet power unit, as the belts make far less noise than conventional chains. Engine noise is also lessened through the use of water cooling, with the radiator mounted across the front down tubes.

To keep the bike manageable in town, Honda placed the engine low in the frame. To compliment this, the gas tank is under the seat; what appears to be the gas tank is a lockable "cabinet" containing the radiator-overflow tank and electrics.

Throughout the remainder of the 1970s a number of revisions were made. These included Comstar wheels, a revised exhaust system, and an unusual, auxiliary instrument cluster mounted on the "gas tank." The most significant change, came in the spring of 1980, when Honda announced yet another variant of the popular four.

This much-refined descendant sports a capacity of 1085cc and is known as the GL1100. Gone are the early handling faults caused by a marginal suspension. Instead, the new GL can be described as faultless. The old suspension units were replaced by a new and more effective air-assisted system.

In the GL1100 the engine has also been uprated to give more power and torque. Displacement was increased merely by enlarging the bore 3mm. Larger crankshaft journals cope with the extra output. At the rear of the engine, where there used to be a removable kickstarter, now lies a breakerless electronic-ignition unit, instead of the previous points system. The ignition provides a vacuum advance, and, as a result, hesitation at low speeds has been eradicated.

Performance is hardly staggering, but considering the weight involved, acceleration is quite impressive. The GL1100 will whisk the rider as smoothly as is possible right up to a top speed of 128 mph. Not the fastest in its class, but none too shabby. The five-speed gearbox feeds power to a final drive with an overall ratio slightly lower than previous models. This makes for better acceleration in each gear, but the engine still retains the flexibility the touring rider needs.

Until the introduction of the GL1100, the Gold Wing was criticized for its inadequate damping, a fact made worse by the enormous weight. Honda has resolved the problem with air suspension at both front and rear. The change in the ride is incredible. Not only has the ride improved, but the bike now handles admirably with greater ground clearance as well. The bike is still a heavyweight, but with the suspension improvements the GL1100 has lost many of its predecessor's less-agreeable traits.

A 1978 American spec GL1000 Gold Wing.

above Most of the GL1000's weight is concentrated lower down, making it easy to handle.

left The traditional site for the gas tank is taken instead by the radiator-overflow tank, fuel filler, a small storage tray and a tool kit. The gas tank is under the seat.

Specification

(1980 model)

engine
Water-cooled, four-stroke, flat-four. 75mm (2.95 in.) bore X 61mm (2.4 in.) stroke = 1085cc (66 cu.in.). Compression ratio 9.2:1. Two valves per cylinder operated via rockers by a single overhead camshaft per head. Four sidedraft 30mm Keihin constant-vacuum carburetors

transmission
Five-speed gearbox.
Shaft drive

frame
Duplex cradle

suspension
Front - Showa telescopic air forks
Rear - Swingarm with air-assisted Showa FVQ shocks

brakes
Front - Twin Honda discs
Rear - Single Honda disc

weight
639 lbs. (290kg)

performance
Maximum speed 128mph
Fuel consumption approximately 42 mpg

Successor to the GL1000, the GL1100 incorporated several improvements.

KAWASAKI Z1-RTC TURBO

From its introduction in 1973 and for five years after, the Kawasaki Z-1 reigned supreme as king of the stoplight bandits. Some people bought Zs for looks, a few bought them for reliability, and maybe a few misguided souls bought them for their handling, but everyone who bought one expected and got the hardest accelerating motorcycle in production. Oh, it may have softened a bit over the years, lost some of the crisp response of the original 903cc machine, but no machine had matched its straightline performance.

All that changed in 1978. Honda, Yamaha and Suzuki introduced one-liter-class superbikes, and each of them was faster than the Kawasaki. Not only was the king no longer the king, the big Z wasn't even crown prince.

Enter Alan Masek. At one time a vice president of Kawasaki of America, Masek offered to buy 1000 1978 Z1-Rs from the Kawasaki factory, with the intention of regaining the crown through the magic of turbocharging. At the time the cafe styling of the Z1-R was as popular as muddy boots, so Kawasaki

gave the nod. Masek contacted John Gleason of American Turbo Pak, who promptly put together the package. Not officially involved, the people at Kawasaki covered their faces and peeked through their fingers.

ATP dumped the Mikuni carburetors and the four-into-two exhaust system, then bolted on a Rajay turbocharger, collector exhaust and a Bendix accelerator-pump carburetor. The installation was well thought out and exceptionally neat.

The result was a coldblooded, ill-tempered brute described by Michael Jordan as the type of machine best chained to the floor and fed chunks of raw meat—specifically children and puppies. With the standard Kawasaki chassis, a horsepower increase from "too much" to "*way* too much" made the bike a handful in anything but a straight line. But in a straight line, the Z1-R TC achieved its purpose. Quarter-mile time dipped well below 11 seconds and the crown returned, albeit through the back door, to the house of Kawasaki.

It takes an experienced hand to use the perfor-

The turbocharged engine of the Z1-R TC.

mance of the Turbo, and an even more experienced one to stay out of trouble with it. Without boost, the engine is nothing more than a stock Z with a single carburetor. The oversize turbo makes low-speed throttle response poor, despite the stock compression and the "pumper" carburetor. When cold, the engine burbles, spits and belches for the first five minutes of running.

All that changes when the boost comes on. Horsepower goes from perhaps 10% less than stock to approximately 40% more than stock. Clichés like "explosive power," "rocket-like acceleration," "white-knuckle ride" and "getting in over your head" take on new meaning. This machine was made for one purpose, and when the boost comes on there's no mistaking that purpose.

Boost is limited to 6 psi, and pressures over 8 psi are not recommended for long periods without extensive engine mods, i.e., welding the crankshaft. Surprisingly, the engine holds up quite well when these restrictions are followed, which is nice to know—there's no engine warranty.

The rest of the machine is standard Z1-R. The same powerful, cross-drilled disc brakes, two front, one rear; same angular styling with the short bikini fairing; the same decent chassis and the same marginal shocks. Although not the Turbo's forte, handling could be described as adequate—if the bike's not pushed. That's something akin to describing a bike's weather-proofing as "good, if kept garaged."

In total, 1600 of these machines were produced in 1978 and '79, and that's all there is; there ain't no more. Most of those around are probably low-mileage machines—it's hard to cover a lot of distance 1/4-mile at a time.

The Z1-R TC may look normal enough, but all normality is left behind when the boost comes on.

above The original turbocharger installation was an exceptionally neat package.

opposite The standard Z1-R provided the basic body for the turbocharged version.

Specification

(1979 model)

engine
Air-cooled, four-stroke, four-cylinder. 70mm (2.75 in.) bore X 66mm (2.6 in.) stroke = 1015cc (62 cu.in.). Maximum power approximately 125 bhp at 8000 rpm. Compression ratio 8.7:1. Two valves per cylinder operated directly by twin overhead camshafts. One 38mm Bendix carburetor with Rayjay turbocharger

transmission
Five-speed gearbox. Chain drive

frame
Duplex cradle
suspension
Front - Kayaba telescopic fork
Rear - Swingarm with Kayaba coil-over shocks
brakes
Front - Twin Kawasaki discs
Rear - Single Kawasaki disc
weight
495 lbs. (225kg)
performance
Maximum speed—who knows?
Fuel consumption—who cares?

HARLEY-DAVIDSON FLT TOUR GLIDE

right The Harley Davidson FLT Tour Glide of 1980.

At first glance, the 1980 Tour Glide looks like last year's Electra Glide—or the year before, or the year before that or.... It's not. This bike is the most improved machine to come from Milwaukee since the Duo Glide in 1958.

Complimenting a new five-speed transmission and frame-mounted fairing is an entirely new frame. Gone is the old "Flexi-Flier" handling, the ponderous feel and miniscule lean angles of the FLH. Starting with a clean slate and a sharp pencil, Harley-Davidson designed a strong boxed-section frame that uses rubber mounts and aircraft-type spherical joints to isolate and steady the engine. The mounting arrangement is quite similar to the Norton "Isolastic" system, but updated about ten years.

In addition to its new engine mounting, front-end geometry has been completely revised. The forks *appear* to be mounted "backwards," that is, the fork tubes are mounted behind the steering neck. The triple clamps are also offset to increase rake and trail without producing the high steering effort and large turning radius normally associated with this type of steering geometry. This fork layout compliments the normal gyroscopic forces that stabilize the bike at high speed, but at the same time reduces the low-speed awkwardness often associated with bikes of this size.

Hustling an Electra Glide down a winding road was enough to put your heart in your throat, but not so with a Tour Glide. The FLT is far more poised than its older counterpart. While Harley-Davidson's description of the bike as a "sports tourer" may be stretching the point, the machine may be thrown into corners with much more confidence than with previous models.

The remainder of the specifications point out that the major purpose of the machine is touring. A fully enclosed rear drive provides a low-cost compromise between the efficiency and simplicity of chain final drive and the low maintenance of a shaft. Electronic ignition reduces the frequency of tune-ups while hydraulic tappets, standard on the big twin since 1957, eliminate the need for valve adjustments.

The big 'Glides have always been somewhat ponderous on acceleration, and the FLT preserves this tradition. Requiring more than 15 seconds to cover a standing start quarter mile, the machine would be left in a cloud of tire smoke by any of a dozen machines with half its displacement. The engine

was made for thumping over miles of superhighway at a sedate pace, and this it can do with almost tedious ease. Fuel mileage reflects the machine's intentions, often exceeding 50 mpg.

The machine is not, however, without problems. The triple disc brakes, while reasonably effective, require an inordinate amount of effort to stop the 770-lb. machine. The huge 5.10 X 16-in. tires help give the machine a staggering 455-lb. load capacity, but their major contribution to handling is to keep the attractive cast-aluminum wheels off the ground.

Oh well, at least they've got the right idea.

left The new-look instrument panel.

Twin headlamps have been incorporated into the newly designed fairing.

An entirely new frame and a five-speed gearbox are just two of many changes made on the Tour Glide.

Specification

(1980 model)

engine
Air-cooled, four-stroke, V-twin. 88.8mm (3.50 in.) bore X 108mm (4.25 in.) stroke = 1340cc. (82 cu.in.). Maximum power not available. Compression ratio 8:1. Two valves per cylinder operated via pushrods and rockers by a single central camshaft. One 38mm Keihin carburetor

transmission
Five-speed gearbox. Chain drive

suspension
Front - Showa telescopic forks
Rear - Swingarm with Showa coil-over shocks

frame
Boxed-section backbone, duplex cradle

brakes
Front - Twin Kelsey-Hayes discs
Rear - Single Kelsey-Hayes disc

weight
770 lbs. (350kg)

performance
Maximum speed 98mph
Fuel economy approximately 50 mpg

INDEX

PHOTOS